lonely planet

The
JOY
of
Exploring
Gardens

Contents

Americas

Asia

Europe

Oceania

Introduction

Do more of what you love. This was the inspiration behind the creation of this book – a clarion call that has been part of the Lonely Planet ethos since the company's genesis. Gardens, of course, are loved for as many reasons as there are garden-lovers – for beauty, for science and horticulture, for quiet, for perfume, for the skill and commitment shown by gardeners who have planted seeds and waited months, years and sometimes decades for the payoff. When it comes down to it, we believe gardens are loved for how they make us *feel*, whether it's excited, awed, inspired, serene, exhilarated, rejuvenated, joyful.

This book presents 180 amazing gardens from all over the world. The main criteria for inclusion? The joy we believe you will experience. We feature some of the most famous gardens in the world for this reason – Monet's House and Garden, the High Line, and the Jardin Majorelle are well-known (and well visited) and are always extraordinarily joyful places to explore. Many of the gardens are more unusual, however – in these pages you'll discover a Barbadian sinkhole filled with tropical flowers (Hunte's Gardens); an Austrian palace garden where trick fountains squirt you with water (Hellbrunn Palace Gardens); and a piece of wasteland turned beautiful garden of grief in Sydney (Wendy's Secret Garden). In turn, these places uplift, thrill and inspire.

Our definition of a garden is a broad one. Botanical gardens captivate for the intriguing species they harbour. Marvels of Renaissance design provoke wonder. Yet, we have also included an ecosanctuary in New Zealand that is letting an area of forest return to its pre-human state (Zealandia Te Māra a Tāne), as well as a vast sculpture garden in India constructed by one man out of things other people have thrown away (Nek Chand's Rock Garden). There is not a flower bed in sight in these two gardens, and yet we think they are utterly enchanting.

Joy, like any feeling, is subjective, and while we are confident these gardens can't fail to cheer, this book is also a reminder that opportunities to follow a passion for exploring gardens are everywhere, whether it means seeking out green spaces on your travels or closer to home.

How to use this book

This book presents 60 feature gardens from all over the world organised by region, each accompanied by two more suggestions of great gardens that are similar or nearby. The feature profiles provide at-a-glance reasons to go, plus the optimal month or months to visit. We tell the story of the garden – why it is special, its history, its challenges and the quality of joy you may feel while you're there, and we list three 'don't miss' experiences. In the Q&A panel, you can read the insights and thoughts of experts closely associated with the garden. Alternatively, the My Garden Joy panel gives a personal account of the delight experienced by the writer of the piece. Then, to help you start planning your trip, there is a factbox detailing how to get there, how accessible the site is, and how the garden changes through the year. Check the index to find gardens listed by country and type.

By Dora Whitaker

Foreword

By Lyanda Lynn Haupt

Think of the usual language that we use when speaking of gardens – words like peace, beauty, stillness, wonder. Quiet words of contemplation and tranquillity. This new Lonely Planet volume is different. The promise here, boldly proclaimed, is JOY. Linking joy to gardens is more revolutionary than it seems on the surface. In our online world of memes, the popular suggestion to 'follow your joy' has become a diminishing cliché. But when we step into the garden, our devices quietened (or ideally left behind), the profound depth of that word is allowed to rise around and within us.

Stanley Kunitz, the 10th US poet laureate, was an avid gardener, and his poetry was ever-inspired by the graced whole of a garden, what he called the 'wild braid' of creation. 'I associate the garden with the whole experience of being alive,' he wrote, 'and so, there is nothing in the range of human experience that is separate from what the garden can signify in its eagerness and its insistence, and in its driving energy to live – to grow, to bear fruit.' Joy!

This is not to say that quiet wonders have no place. They absolutely do. In the 'driving energy to live' there is always the complete circle of life. All growth and beauty springs from a fruition that is followed by an essential gathering in – a crinkling of leaves, a return to soil, a release of seed pods going home to the dark and waiting earth where they will lie fallow until the seasonal wheel begins anew its necessary, joyful turning.

I am a nature writer by profession – my books and thoughts typically explore the wilder places beyond gardens, rather than gardens themselves. But being schooled in wilderness has taught me the necessity of the liminal space that gardens offer – a threshold, a passageway into wilder ways of seeing and knowing. Before you can go off the beaten path, after all, you have to be on a path. The garden is that path, that wild connector. We all find our own unique forms of joy in the garden. Here are just a few of the most essential.

The joy of nature's borders

Words evolve much in the same way plants and animals do – through sudden mutations in usage, geographic isolation of speakers, and slow change over time. Words are as alive as birds. And so, in thinking about the wild joy of gardens, it makes sense to wander back through the cobbled pathways of Middle English, back further into Old North French and Middle High German, all the way to Medieval Latin where there emerged a new kind of place upon Earth: the gardinium. The word itself used to have nothing to do with plants, but rather the walls that contained them. The gardinium was an enclosure. Think of ancient monastic gardens, with their arched cloisters where contemplatives would tend growing things – a moving meditating upon the sacred. The aliveness of these places was entirely literal – much-needed herbal medicine and nourishing

food grew alongside flowers and shrubs. All of this was kept enclosed – 'gardened' – within walls that protected against the ever-present possibility of theft, armed conflict, or perhaps even wolves.

You will explore medieval walled gardens in these pages, but whether a garden is literally enclosed or not, it is bordered. One can be within the garden or without it. Within it? We are surrounded by nature, yet set apart. Such a rare gift! For a time we are free to dwell, to rest, to dance in a place beyond the ordinary where leafy shadows guide our steps and everyday cares cannot reach us.

The joy of rootedness

Stone, rain, sand, soil. Wood, bud, grass, cloud. In the garden we are touched by every element. Are you in a desert garden with no water in sight? Remember that beloved Vietnamese Buddhist monk Thich Nhat Hanh teaches us to see as a poet would see: everything we can hold in our hands – every leaf, every feather, every pebble – has come to us through processes of sun, rain, and rock working upon one another through the passage of time. In the garden we press our feet to the earth, our cheek

"For a time we are free to dwell, to rest, to dance in a place beyond the ordinary"

to the bark, our ear to the sky and rediscover that we, too, are made of the fine things: soil, water, sun, bone, stardust. In the garden, we are rooted and at home in nature's ever-turning cycles.

The joy of co-creation

A garden is the deepest of co-creations between humans and nature. When I lived in Japan many years ago, I was fortunate to study with one of Kyoto's most prominent teachers of ikebana – the ancient art of flower arrangement. Students learn early on that arrangements are anchored by three stems of various lengths – a tall one representing the heavens, a shorter one representing the Earth, and one, the middle stem, representing the human presence in balance between these two. We've all been in so-called gardens in which the plants seem forced to meet a pre-conceived sense of order, with shrubs lined up and trimmed into submission. Such places cannot rightly be called gardens at all – they are simply landscaping. The gardens in this volume vary from the overtly designed to the riotously naturalistic, but all of them strike that inspired balance where the human hand is present as humble co-creator with the wild earth. (Another fun etymological aside: the words humble and human are both rooted in the Latin word humus – of the soil.)

The joy of reciprocity

Humans are part of the wild to be sure, but distant wild places are more or less indifferent to our presence. This is not so with gardens, which are created with wandering humans in mind. We bend to the garden's aliveness, and the garden to us. We are on equal footing – each in need of the other for a particular kind of sustenance. Every time I leave a garden – whether I step beyond a cloistered wall, walk through a simple wooden gate, or simply place my feet beyond the last scruff of gravel path, I always turn back to take in one last look. To breathe in the unique fragrance of succulent, or honeysuckle, or

pinyon. To still my heart and listen for the last tendrils of beyond-human voices that accompanied my time there: hummingbird, brush-footed fritillary, the unique language of large stones. Always I know that though I have removed nothing tangible, still I take something with me ≠ that whether I entered the garden while distracted or moody or meditative or skipping the paths, I emerge changed, having received a dear gift. The garden's sweet and rare co-creation between human and soil has worked on and within me. And I like to think, too, that I have offered something back to the garden world – in attentive footsteps, in the wild exchange of breath and presence and delight and imagination.

A garden without a wanderer is a lonely thing. We find joy together.

Lyanda Lynn Haupt is an author, naturalist, ecophilosopher, and speaker whose work explores the complicated connections between humans and the natural world. Her newest book is *Rooted: Life at the Crossroads of Science, Nature, and Spirit.*

Far left: Pathway into the living landscape of Tokachi Millennium Forest, Japan

Left: Co-creation at work in the kitchen garden at Babylonstoren, South Africa

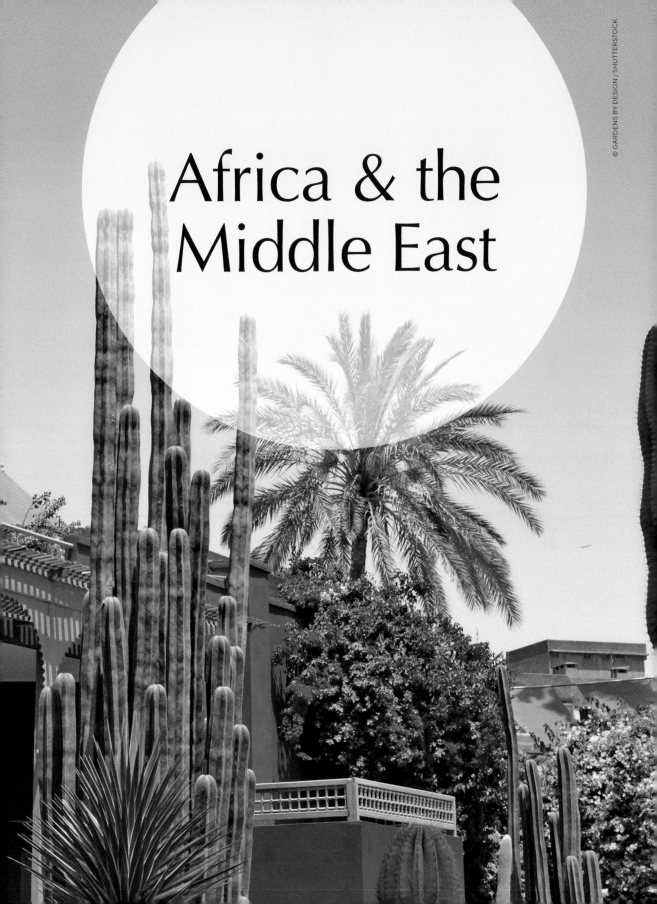

Africa & the Middle East

Wander through a living canvas at Jardin Majorelle

 Inspiration, bold colours, water features

 April and May

MOROCCO

Created by French artist Jacques Majorelle (1886–1962), this unique walled garden takes its inspiration from traditional Moroccan garden design but has a singular aesthetic, courtesy of its vibrant colour palette and seductive, striking plantings.

An artist's creation

When Majorelle decided to create a garden in his newly adopted home of Marrakesh he was in good artistic company – Claude Monet had worked on his garden at Giverny for four decades, Vanessa Bell and Duncan Grant were creating the garden at Charleston in East Sussex and Frida Kahlo would soon begin her transformation of the garden at the Casa Azul in Mexico City. Majorelle's garden soon became one of the artist's greatest passions and legacies, something that was immediately apparent to fashion designer Yves Saint Laurent and his business partner Pierre Bergé when they acquired the property in the 1980s, two decades after its creator's death. Majorelle's achievement was extraordinary, conjuring a lush and colour-saturated oasis from a searingly hot and arid landscape. This is a garden that is a true haven, one that takes inspiration from classical Islamic gardens, which use water and shade to soothe both the body and the spirit. Anchored by an elongated reflection pond, the garden's other water features include a gently playing fountain and a romantic lily pond populated with paddling terrapins.

Right: There are over 300 plant species in the garden, including rare cacti

Below: Majorelle's art deco studio is now a museum of Berber culture; the painter loved dazzling contrast

© COURTESY OF JARDIN MAJORELLE

My Garden Joy

Anyone who has visited Marrakesh will understand when I say that the city is a place where sensory overload is the norm. Every time I travel here I feel as if I have been transported into a vortex of sound, smell and experiences. Pungent aromas waft from the food stands in the souks, the evocative but loud strains of the call to prayer issue from ancient minarets and a swirling mass of humanity converges every night to party on the Djemaa El Fna – all are wonderful but can be overwhelming. In contrast, the first time I walked into the Jardin Majorelle I immediately felt soothed by the greenery, the water and the tranquil surrounds. And the Majorelle Blue is truly wondrous; for me, it is the perfect representation of Morocco's vivid and extraordinarily beguiling beauty.
Virginia Maxwell

© COURTESY OF JARDIN MAJORELLE

Jardin Majorelle

Bold colours

The water features and luxuriant green foliage – which includes a bamboo forest, fan palms, date palms and *Monstera deliciosa* – may induce a sense of calm, but the use of vibrant and boldly contrasting colours elsewhere has the opposite effect, stimulating the senses and reminding the visitor that the garden's creator had an artist's eye. The signature colour used here, an arresting shade of cobalt blue inspired by Majorelle's travels throughout Morocco, was patented by the artist and given his name. His studio is painted in this Majorelle Blue, as are the fountain and the edges of the ponds. The paths that loop across the garden are painted a rich red, pots are citrus yellow and powder blue, and walls and trellises are covered in masses of shocking pink bougainvillea. Exploring here is akin to walking through a gallery full of bold canvases that pique the senses and the mind.

Opposite: Bahia Palace in Arabic translates as 'brilliance'

Right and below: Primary colours accentuate the green of the plants; the lotus and water lily pond

© COURTESY OF JARDIN MAJORELLE

Botanical riches

Majorelle planted his garden with exotic botanical specimens sourced from across the globe, and Saint Laurent and Bergé carried on this legacy. Working with Moroccan ethnobotanist Abderrazzak Benchaabane, they renewed original plantings and also sourced an amazing array of cacti and succulents from the Americas. Some of these are tall, some squat, all are spiky. Other plantings include jasmine, which imparts a suitably sensuous smell to its surrounds.

Don't Miss

➞ **Watching the terrapins in the lily pond**

➞ **Sipping mint tea in the courtyard cafe**

➞ **Visiting the Berber Museum housed in Majorelle's studio**

Find Your Joy

Getting there
The garden is in Marrakesh's Gueliz district, a short taxi ride or a 2-mile (3.2km) walk from Djemaa El Fna.

Accessibility
The garden is wheelchair accessible.

When to go
Come in April or May, when the bougainvillea and orange blossom flower, or in September, when the scent of jasmine fills the air. Avoid the heat of high summer (June to August) if possible.

Further information
• Admission charge.
• Open daily, year-round.
• No dogs allowed.

• Courtyard cafe on-site.
• www.jardinmajorelle. com

© GLADSKIKH TATIANA / SHUTTERSTOCK

Other Marrakesh Gardens

Bahia Palace

This compound of exquisitely decorated riads (traditional townhouses set around an internal garden) dates from the late 19th century. It includes two traditional courtyards decorated with ceramic tiles and fountains, and a large rectangular garden with lush plantings of orange and banana trees, lilies and yellow 'painted bamboo.'

Don't miss

Savouring the sweet scent of orange blossom in the garden of the Petit Riad during March

Dar Si Said

Now home to the Museum of Moroccan Arts, this 19th-century *dar* (traditional townhouse with a tiled internal courtyard) is unusual in that it also has a riad-style garden planted with citrus trees, palms, flowering shrubs and lilies. In the centre of the garden is a central fountain sheltered by an intricately decorated wooden kiosk.

Don't miss

The Angel's trumpet (*Brugmansia arborea*) in bloom between May and early September

Find harmony in Haifa's holy gardens

ISREAL

♡ Unity, symmetry, nature's diversity

🕐 April to June

A shining red-golden dome sits at the top of a kind of stairway to heaven. You climb one step after another, passing immaculate terraced gardens, with the sparkling Mediterranean below – it can only be Haifa's breathtaking Baha'i Gardens. A symphony of floral colours and scents are revealed at every turn. The silence, rare in this industrial city, is only broken by the sound of flowing water from a lotus-flower-shaped fountain. It's clear this is no ordinary garden but a place of pilgrimage and peace.

Persian roots

The future location of the gardens on the slopes of Mt Carmel was chosen in 1891 by Bahá'u'lláh, founder of the Baha'i faith. Bahá'u'lláh, originally from Persia, was exiled to the Ottoman Empire for his teachings and later buried in nearby Akko. The early gardens and shrines were designed a few decades later in the 1950s by his grandson, Shoghi Effendi, but the landscaped terraces were only completed in 2001 by Persian architect Fariborz Sahba, designer of the Lotus Temple in Delhi. Strolling around these 'Hanging Gardens of Haifa', the Persian influence is palpable. Emerald-green mosaics, Arabic inscriptions and ornamental urns adorn the Shrine of the Bab. Small courtyards blend the outdoors with the indoors. And shade is provided by olive, citrus and pomegranate trees.

Global gardens

Yet, with a closer look, there's a more global aspect to these gardens and

Right: Timeless elegance: the garden mixes neo-classical and Persian design

Below: The gardens comprise 19 terraces representing the first disciples of the Bab

© DMITRIY FELDMAN SVARSHIK / SHUTTERSTOCK

© © LEONID ANDRONOV / SHUTTERSTOCK

This place represents more than a garden, right?
Right. It's the spiritual and administrative centre of the Baha'i Council, and several thousand pilgrims come every year. But we maintain these gardens for everyone.

How does it reflect its different influences?
The older parts have a formal European influence, with hedges, lawns and trees. The newer terraces, where the running water feels like a river running down a mountain, are similar to Persian designs.

You've been recycling your green waste since the 1950s.
Yes, all the lawn clippings, flower cuttings and leaves are turned into compost or mulch and reused.

What's mulch?
It's a covering that hasn't been composted yet. It protects the soil from erosion and temperature changes, conserves water and slows the growth of weeds.

What's your favourite spot?
The ancient trees. I'm biased towards forests.

Darlene Robinson,
Chief Horticulturist

Right: The Baha'i Gardens of Akko feature a bold geometric design

Left: The gardens are planted with species that require little water, such as aloe camperi

© MARAT LALA / SHUTTERSTOCK

Don't Miss

→ Being dazzled by the shrine's terraces lit up at night

→ Taking in the views of Haifa Bay

→ Meditating under a circle of old cypress trees

their over 450 plant types. The green lawns bordered by trimmed hedges recall an English garden. Canary Island date palms adorn each terrace on either side of the Odessa-esque steps. Exotic elements like cacti, bonsai trees and the spiky bird of paradise flower (native of South Africa) add to the international feel. The white-marble Universal House of Justice building closely resembles the Parthenon in Greece. And the Shrine at the heart of the complex – a mix of mosque, church and Indian temple – has stained-glass and a Portuguese-tiled dome.

Digging deeper

The symmetry of the gardens is particularly striking – each side of the stairway is a mirror image of its opposite counterpart, creating a sense of equality, one of the cores of the Baha'i faith. Elsewhere there are circular flower beds – signifying our one planet that orbits the sun and holds all humans together – and spectacular nine-pointed star flower beds. Nine is the holiest number to the Baha'i, hence the Shrine of the Bab is nine-sided with nine doors.

It seems every feature has a deeper meaning. 'The world of humanity is like a garden and the various races are the flowers', says Nabil, the garden administrator, quoting a Baha'i teaching. 'These gardens represent the transformation that we want to see in the world.' With these thoughts in mind, whatever your beliefs, you can't help but leave with a sense of healing and hope.

Find Your Joy

Getting there
The nearest train station is Haifa Center HaShmona. From there, take bus 58 or a short taxi ride to Yefe Nof St.

Accessibility
The gardens include a short section with a moderate slope that's accessible for wheelchairs from Hatzionut Ave. The visitor centre has an accessible auditorium and toilet, the tour guides are trained to lip-read and visually impaired visitors can bring service animals.

When to go
In late spring (May and June) the blooming jacaranda flowers paint the gardens in purple rain. In December the citrus trees bear fruit and the gardens provide the backdrop to Haifa's Christmas market on Ben Gurion Blvd.

Further information
• Free admission; booking required for upper terraces tours.
• Open year-round except Baha'i holidays and Yom Kippur.
• No dogs allowed, except assistance dogs.
• Visitors must dress modestly (shoulders covered).
• There's a visitor centre but no cafe.
• www.ganbahai.org.il

Other Gardens in Israel

Baha'i Gardens of Akko

The no-less-impressive sister of Haifa's Baha'i Gardens is further north along the coast in the city of Akko. It was here that Bahá'u'lláh died in 1892 and was buried in a house adjacent to an old Ottoman mansion called Al-Bahjá (Place of Delight). The approach to the shrine is down a long, straight path that leads to a circular garden.

Don't miss

Paying your respects to the glorious 1200-year-old sycamore fig tree

Jerusalem Botanical Gardens

West of Jerusalem's Old City, these 30 acres of gardens are divided into six sections representing different regions of the world. They were founded in 1931 by Belarusian Alexander Eig, chairman of the Hebrew University botany department. Today, it's being revived as a much-needed garden of peace in a troubled city.

Don't miss

Wandering the Tropical Conservatory with endangered plants and a variety of orchids

Soak up the views in South Africa's signature garden

SOUTH AFRICA

♡ Mountain vistas, rare flora, uplifting hikes

🕐 August to November

If you could click your fingers and magic up a garden encompassing all of South Africa's diverse wonders, you would end up with something a lot like Kirstenbosch. This legendary botanical garden is abuzz with wildlife, alive with unique plants and blooms and framed by the jagged and familiar profile of South Africa's most famous summit.

With Table Mountain presiding over the scene like a benevolent deity, you'll feel like an early botanist on safari in this green bower – one of the first botanical gardens to make a mission of protecting local plant life. Today, it harbours over 7000 of South Africa's native species. Enter and feel your pulse tangibly slow as the noise of Cape Town melts away to a murmur.

Innovative garden philosophy
At a time when botanic gardens across the globe were filling their arboretums with imports, the directors of Kirstenbosch saw the value in South Africa's bounteous local flora. In this leafy expanse, you'll submerge in five of South Africa's six biomes, covering everything from savanna to fynbos, the unique ecosystem of the southern Cape.

Accordingly, the garden's big-hitter species are the alien-looking Proteaceae and Ericaceae of the fynbos, with their drought-adapted leaves and bristle-brush flowers, and the spear-flowered aloes and spiky cycads of the Karoo desert. In many gardens, plants are exotic but familiar; in Kirstenbosch, there's a feeling of stepping into another world, like Mars imagined by 1950s sci-fi artists.

© STEPHEN B. GOODWIN / SHUTTERSTOCK

Right: Back from the dead: whorled heath lost its former habitat as Cape Town expanded

Below: The epic backdrop of Table Mountain; a sunbird meets a protea flower

© WANDERING VIEWS / SHUTTERSTOCK

Q&A

What makes Kirstenbosch special?
Kirstenbosch grows only plants that are indigenous to southern Africa, many of which are in danger of extinction. The whorled heath was presumed extinct in the 1980s, but our horticulturists tracked down eight surviving specimens and re-introduced the species into the wild.

Clever. What's it like having Table Mountain as a neighbour?
There are no fences between Kirstenbosch and the Table Mountain National Park, so the garden merges seamlessly with the park. And we have a lot of wildlife, some resident, some visiting to feed or breed.

Go on then, make us jealous.
I love the cobbled pathways in the older parts of Kirstenbosch that lead to quiet corners and unexpected viewpoints. I also love the wild, un-gardened parts of Kirstenbosch, one of the few places where natural forest is so close to civilisation.

Alice Notten, Interpretation Officer

© FINN STOCK / SHUTTERSTOCK

© ISPYVENUS / SHUTTERSTOCK

Kirstenbosch National Botanical Garden

Opposite: The abundant coastal fynbos of Harold Porter Botanical Gardens

Right: The greatest show on earth? A concert venue shelters below Table Mountain

© SANDRA MORI / SHUTTERSTOCK

An accidental wonder

This haven of biodiversity emerged from unpromising beginnings. The first garden on the site was a straggle of almond trees and brambles planted by the Dutch to protect the Cape colony from intruders. By the time Henry Harold Pearson, the founder of Kirstenbosch, arrived on the scene in 1913, the land was overrun by weeds and wild pigs.

Pearson started as he meant to go on, planting native cycads, shooing off the pesky pigs and setting the groundwork for one of the world's great botanical collections. When he died from malaria just three years later, he was buried in Kirstenbosch with the epitaph 'If ye seek his monument, look around.'

Where garden meets mountain

You can't talk about Kirstenbosch without talking about Table Mountain. As you stroll through this heart-stopping garden, you'll feel Cape Town's godfather mountain calling like a siren. If you come to view the plant life and don't also tack on a hike to the summit, you're missing a trick.

The other way to get above it all at Kirstenbosch is on the Boomslang, a sinuous, skeletal canopy walkway that lifts you up above the treetops. Ribbon-tailed sugar birds flit through the undergrowth, and the smells of Africa – herbs, chlorophyll, dust and blossom – waft around like perfume. At times Kirstenbosch feels more nature reserve than human-created garden, just another part of its magic.

Don't Miss

→ Admiring vistas of Table Mountain

→ Traversing the touchy-feely fragrance garden

→ Listening to a Kirstenbosch Summer Sunset Concert on a balmy Sunday

Find Your Joy

Getting there

Kirstenbosch sits on the eastern side of Table Mountain in the suburb of Newlands. Hop-on, hop-off city sightseeing buses run regularly to the gardens, or there's a weekday bus from Mowbray Station.

Accessibility

Despite the steep gradients, all visitor facilities can accommodate wheelchairs, and the Braille trail and fragrance garden were created with the visually impaired in mind. However, some areas have steps or paths that are too steep for the mobility impaired.

When to go

Something is in flower or showing its best foliage at Kirstenbosch every month of the year, but the best time for blooms is August to November, when the fynbos explodes into a firework display of colour. The lively Kirstenbosch Summer Sunset Concert season runs from November to April.

Further information

• Admission charge.
• Open daily, year-round.
• No dogs allowed.
• Cafe on site.
• www.sanbi.org/gardens/kirstenboch

Other South African Gardens

Walter Sisulu Botanical Garden

Set where Johannesburg melts into the veldt, the Walter Sisulu Botanical Garden feels like an enchanted glade. Trees thrust their arms skywards, lawns glow tree-frog green, and a crystal waterfall gushes over a rocky cleft at the head of the valley. More than 240 bird species have been spotted here.

Don't miss

The chance to picnic by the falls and let raucous Jo'burg slip from your consciousness

Harold Porter Botanical Gardens

If Kirstenbosch has got you in the fynbos mood, head to the eastern end of False Bay, where these gardens nestle between rocky outcrops and the South Atlantic. Forests hide inside rocky gorges, dunes give way to blonde sand and waterfalls tip into limpid pools, stained tea-red by the fynbos vegetation.

Don't miss

The wildlife – you'll share this emerald escape with porcupines, hyraxes and baboons

© ANNA OM / SHUTTERSTOCK

Sample some paradise at the Bagh-e Fin

♡ Water features, tranquillity, architecture

🕐 May

IRAN

Like the luxuriant carpets for which Persia has always been renowned, the traditional Persian garden is arranged on a rigidly symmetrical grid, features repetitive elements and incorporates trees, flowers and fountains. Aesthetically refined and virtuosic in its water engineering, this is one of the most ancient and influential forms of garden design, one that was formally acknowledged by Unesco, when nine important and historic Iranian gardens were added to the World Heritage List in 2011. Though not the oldest of the Persian Gardens included in that listing, the Bagh-e Fin, an exquisite evocation of an earthly paradise set in otherwise inhospitable and arid desert surrounds 125 miles (200km) north of the city of Esfahan, is perhaps the most beautiful and unexpected.

Safavid splendour

After Abbas the Great, the fifth Safavid Shah of Iran, came to the throne in 1588 he moved the imperial capital to Esfahan and embarked on a major building program there. The public squares, mosques, madrasahs, bridges and palaces that resulted are among Iran's greatest treasures, as are the pleasure gardens he commissioned in the city and its region. Entering the Bagh-e Fin, you are presented with a veritable Eden enclosed by high mud-and-adobe walls. Designed according to the classical Persian Chahar Bagh (Four Gardens) model, the lush garden features four planted geometric

Right: Natural water pressure powers the many bubbling fountains

Below: The archetypal *chahar bagh* (quadrilateral Persian garden); a sun-drenched pavilion

My Garden Joy

The shahs believed that creating a beautiful garden was an act of religious reverence. I'm sure that Abbas the Great intended that the Bagh-e Fin should perform this function, but I can't help but conjecture that he might have had another ambition – to prove how powerful he was by taming nature and creating something verdant and cool in the middle of a harsh desert. If that was indeed the case, he succeeded magnificently because my overwhelming feeling upon entering was one of awe at what he and his engineers achieved. But then the beauty of the garden started to work its magic and I realised that, for its creator, technology was no doubt only the means to an end. And that end was to create something beautiful and unexpected and in so doing, celebrate the wonder of life itself.
Virginia Maxwell

Right: The immaculate symmetry of Bagh-e Chehel Sotun

Left and below: Bagh-e Fin's Qajar-era bathhouse; the cooling hue of blue mosaic

the sun, you are soothed by the sound of gently playing fountains and refreshed by water-cooled air. Shelter from the sun is offered in exquisite pleasure pavilions constructed for a series of Safavid- and Qajar-era shahs. It's easy to imagine these powerful people escaping political intrigues and weighty matters of state at court and retreating here for some sorely needed repose.

Don't Miss

→ Admiring water views from the Shotor Galu (Pool House)

→ Marvelling at the decoration of the Qajar-era rear pavilion

→ Enjoying a rosewater ice-cream in the garden teahouse

sections and a handsome water feature representing the pool of life at its centre, surrounded by treelined walkways and a network of gently flowing water channels with no apparent source.

Naturally cool

The pools, fountains and channels in the garden are fed by water that gushes from a nearby hillside spring and is transported here by a system of *qanats*, or underground tunnels. Wandering alongside the network of intersecting water channels lined by glazed turquoise tiles that shimmer in

Clever colours

The garden's water features, cedar trees, box hedges and *karts* (formal flowerbeds) contribute to a colour palette that is predominantly green and blue, promoting an impression of coolness. Kashi cedars, some of which are 500 years old, minimise water evaporation by throwing shade over pools and channels. Other plantings – including orange trees, roses, jasmine and marigolds – impart bursts of colour and infuse the air with paradisical fragrances.

Find Your Joy

Getting there
The garden is located in the village of Fin, 5.5 miles (9km) west of the city of Kashan. Shared and private taxis to Fin depart

from Kamal al-Molk Square in Kashan.

Accessibility
Most of the garden paths are flat and suitable for wheelchairs and the mobility-impaired.

When to go
April and May are the best times to visit, when roses and orange blossom perfume the garden.

Further information
• Admission charge.
• Open daily, year-round.
• No dogs allowed.
• On-site teahouse.

Other Unesco-Listed Persian Gardens

Bagh-e Chehel Sotun

Surrounding the 17th-century Kakh-e Chehel Sotun, a richly decorated pleasure palace and pavilion in central Esfahan, this Unesco-listed classical garden is home to ancient Persian pines (*Pinus Eldarica*), as well as many other tall trees. Its focal point is a large ornamental pool in front of the palace buildings.

Don't miss

Counting the columns of the *talar* (porch) and their reflections in the front pool to see how the Hall of 40 Columns acquired its name

Bagh-e Eram

More densely planted than its co-listees in the Unesco citation, this large rectangular-shaped Persian garden in Shiraz is home to dense plantings of cedars, pines, fruit trees, small decorative trees and annual flowers. Canals running in four directions meet at a large ornamental pool in which the image of a handsome Qajar-era garden pavilion is reflected.

Don't miss

The rose garden with its 300 varieties of sweet-smelling trees

Try the produce at a historically inspired kitchen garden

 Design, views, serenity

 February

There are few sounds as calming as that of rippling water. This is the underlying soundtrack of Babylonstoren, where streams from nearby Simonsberg mountain run down gently graded slopes through ponds planted with edible lotus, nymphaea lilies and *waterblommetjies*, an indigenous winter-flowering plant used in traditional South African cooking. There's poetry here too, both visual and literal – the base of the shallow pool at the centre of the Citrus Garden is decorated with Delft-inspired tiles and lines from an Afrikaans poem by DJ Opperman.

Inspired by historic gardens

The inspiration for Babylonstoren was a similar garden planted in 1652 by the Dutch East India Company when it established a settlement at this southern tip of Africa. Everything in Cape Town's Company's Garden (which still exists) was edible or had medicinal value, and it's the same at Babylonstoren, one of the oldest working farms in the Cape Winelands.

The incredible kitchen gardens follow a 21st-century design by architect Patrice Taravella that draws on his experience of reconstructing a medieval cloistered garden at the Notre Dame d'Orsan monastery in France. Taravella's layout has straight walkways and low hedges framing vegetable patches, fruit orchards, nutteries, a maze of prickly pear cacti and a living archive of rare and indigenous plants such as cycads and clivias.

Right: There are 15 distinct garden areas at Babylonstoren, all filled with edible plants

Below: Simonsberg mountain surveys production; bottle gourds on the vine

Q&A

What's new at Babylonstoren?
We have a new kitchen garden in an area where we used to compost and grow pumpkins. It's been beautifully enclosed by whitewashed stone walls and we are growing more herbs, vegetables and cut flowers.

There's lots of wildlife on the farm. Are there any critters that you don't welcome?
Definitely squirrels. They're like little monkeys, they love nibbling on the pumpkins and on the fruits. They love helping themselves. I had one yesterday, in the cherry tree.

What's special about Babylonstoren?
You don't need to like gardens to enjoy this one. It has so many layers and there are so many stories. I would encourage visitors to do a garden tour or a workshop. At the very least, stop and speak to a gardener.

Liesl van der Walt, Senior Gardener and Head of Tourism Experiences

Babylonstoren

© DOOK / COURTESY OF BABYLONSTOREN

Wake up for the ducks

One of the best ways to enjoy Babylonstoren is to stay overnight. That way you're here to see the 200 or so white Pekin ducks which are released each morning from their pen to waddle their way through the garden, down to the orchards and vineyards. Next be delighted by the five types of chicken that you'll also discover scratching around the grounds.

In spring, keep an eye out for tortoises as they emerge from hibernation ready to mate and hungry for greens and stone fruit. Explore further to find the six different-shaped hives that are homes for the Cape honey bees, which pollinate the garden and provide the sweet amber liquid used in Babylonstoren's restaurant and cafe.

Nest like a bird

Secluded amid tall stands of bamboo is a human-sized nest woven from kubu cane.

Opposite: The Château de Pringins garden bathed in afternoon sun

Right and below: In the pink: strolling beneath fragrant roses; sampling the goods

Climb inside and wait silently to catch sight of birds feasting on sunflower seeds and the sweet purple fruits of a 180-year-old mulberry tree.

Also guaranteed to delight is the sinuous Puff Adder tunnel, made from strips of balau wood on steel frames, which snakes beside a stream shaded by olive and eucalyptus trees. It displays seasonal plants such as fragrant heritage roses in November and the garden's superb collection of clivias in September, gorgeous blooms in every shade of yellow, orange and red.

Don't Miss

→ Navigating to the heart of the prickly pear maze

→ Enjoying the fragrance of rambling roses on the garden's 48 pergolas

→ Strolling barefoot across the chamomile lawn

Find Your Joy

Getting there

You'll need a car to reach Babylonstoren. The estate is in the Cape Winelands, 33 miles (53km) northeast of Cape Town or 14 miles

(23km) south of Paarl via the N1 highway.

Accessibility

Parents with strollers and visitors in wheelchairs may find the gravel paths in the garden tricky to negotiate.

When to go

January and February for peaches, nectarines, prickly pears, figs and grapes; March and April

for pomegranates and olives; mid-September for clivias; late October and November for roses.

Further information

• Admission charge.

• Open year-round.
• No dogs allowed, except assistance dogs.
• Restaurant, cafe and bakery on site.
• www.babylonstoren. com

© COURTESY OF BABYLONSTOREN

Other Kitchen Gardens

Lost Gardens of Heligan, England

These magnificent 19th-century gardens fell into disrepair following WWI, but have been splendidly restored by the team behind the Eden Project. It's a horticultural wonderland encompassing working kitchen gardens, fruit-filled greenhouses, formal lawns, a secret grotto and a massive rhododendron, plus the lost-world 'Jungle' of ferns, palms and tropical blooms.

Don't miss

Snapping a photo of the sleeping woman sculpture

Château de Prangins, Switzerland

This half hectare walled plot is Switzerland's largest historical kitchen garden. The palisade walls create a microclimate for the nearly 200 varieties of fruits, vegetables, aromatic and utilitarian plants which are grown in beds laid out in a cruciform pattern. First created in the 18th century, the garden was restored in 1998. Once a month there are guided tours in English.

Don't miss

Rubbing the leaves in the 'touch' bed and tasting the plants in the 'taste' bed

© TRABANTOS / SHUTTERSTOCK

Step into a piece of Indian Ocean history

 Palms, giant lilies, nostalgia

 May

MAURITIUS

With its swaying palms and supersaturated greenery, the Sir Seewoosagur Ramgoolam Botanical Garden at Pamplemousses feels like stepping inside the reflective facets of an emerald. Even better, this lush garden tells the story of Mauritius in microcosm – a yarn of feuding empires, ambitious fortune hunters and the spice trade, all set under the beating tropical sun.

Horticultural skulduggery
The oldest botanical garden in the southern hemisphere was set up not for beauty but for empire. French governor Mahé de La Bourdonnais planted the first seeds in what was then a humble kitchen garden in 1735, providing fresh fruit and veg for the vitamin-C-starved sailors who endured the trip from mainland France to the speck in the Indian Ocean known as Isle de France.

Sprawling around the veranda-ringed Château Mon Plaisir, the garden emerged as a horticultural battleground in the 1770s, as colonial powers squabbled for control of global spice markets. French botanist Pierre Poivre smuggled in nutmeg and clove plants to break the Dutch trade in spices from the Dutch East Indies (modern-day Indonesia), and Mauritius' importance as a powerhouse on the spice route was assured.

Plantation made garden
Also thank Pierre Poivre for the shady avenues of trees that call like a beacon on days

© MARK GOMEZ / SHUTTERSTOCK

Right: An avenue of bottle palms extends a restorative welcome

Below: Giant water lilies can unfurl to 6.5ft (2m) diameter in a few hours; lotus seeds are an edible treat

© ALTRENDO IMAGES / SHUTTERSTOCK

My Garden Joy

It's raining from a blue sky! This was my first thought as I stepped through the Victorian-era gateway of the Sir Seewoosagur Ramgoolam Botanical Garden for the first time. I was not yet familiar with Mauritius' quirky weather patterns, and the droplets spilling from the sapphire blue lent an extra intensity to the hyperreal greenery. With palm fronds swooshing overhead like enormous green hands, it felt almost fantastical, like the bedroom-grown garden in *Where the Wild Things Are* or the naïve jungles from a Henri Rousseau painting. My other overarching memory is of the pool of giant water lilies – and the inner voice that seemed to dare me to run across, just in case the super-sized leaves could take my weight. I resisted, but it left a profound impression.

Joe Bindloss

© NATALYA STERLEVA / SHUTTERSTOCK

© ANDREITA_PRAGUE / SHUTTERSTOCK

© HEMIS / AWL IMAGES

Right: The triffid-like water banana palm in the Seychelles

Left: The garden was initially established as a vegetable plot for the Château Mon Plaisir

the colonial-era fortune-seekers in powdered wigs, plotting the next rapacious campaign against the island up the road.

An abundance of chlorophyll

Thanks to the moisture-laden trade winds, it's the green punch of the gardens that lingers in the memory. Foliage the intense green of chameleons, pythons and parakeets swishes on all sides, tall palms high-five overhead, and lotuses burst forth from emerald pools. The effect is of a tropical forest that has been pulled apart, giving each plant room to breathe.

On an island that has thrown its all into the pursuit of the perfect beach resort, it's a soul-soothing reminder of the Mauritius that existed before the overwater bungalows. Arrive at opening time outside of the main season, and you'll be able to bask in its green glow with just the swoosh of palm fronds – and the gardens' resident giant tortoises – for company.

Don't Miss

→ Glimpsing the famous giant water lily pond, with its baffle of sky-piercing tropical trees

→ Strolling the avenues of royal palms

→ Meeting the garden's giant Aldabra tortoises

when Mauritius' white sands lose their lustre. The kleptomaniac botanist, and his like-minded successors, filled the estate at Mon Plaisir with plants from every corner of the globe, from spices and Barbadian grapefruit trees to the Amazonian giant lilies that float like life-rafts on the gardens' reflective central pool.

Strolling under the royal and bottle palms that form an honour guard over its walkways, you'll feel a connection with nature, and with the island's history, in a way you'll never feel by the hotel pool. Half squint, and you can almost see

Find Your Joy

Getting there
Pamplemousses sits northeast of Port Louis. Buses run to the gardens regularly from Port Louis' Immigration Square bus

station and Grand Gaube, with less frequent buses from Grand Baie and Trou aux Biches.

Accessibility
The winding paths may deter less mobile visitors from exploring every corner of the gardens, but the terrain is mostly level, and golf buggy tours can be arranged.

When to go
The gardens are at their most beautiful immediately after the rains (December to April), when the greenery glows with intensity. Come from May to November to see the gardens under drier skies but avoid the peak cyclone months of January and February, when tropical storms can blast in from the Indian Ocean.

Further information
• Admission charge.
• Open daily, year-round.
• No dogs allowed.
• There's no cafe, so bring snacks and drinks.
• https://ssrbg.govmu.org

Other Indian Ocean Gardens

Seychelles National Botanical Gardens, Seychelles

With its fanning palms, passion-fruit vines, hibiscus blooms and pitcher plants, the whole of the Seychelles feels like a botanical garden, but the concept is formalised at the National Botanic Gardens near Victoria. Here, palms sashay, orchids flare, and water banana palms burst out of lily ponds like alien life forms.

Don't miss

Hiking the trails of Morne Seychelles National Park, which begin just uphill from the gardens

Jardin de l'État, La Réunion

La Réunion's colonial-era botanic gardens are surrounded by the sprawl of Saint-Denis, but they've been here since the 1760s, when Pierre Poivre starting planting imported trees and spices believed to be 'of use to the colony'. Today, this small but lovely lung spills over with Dr Seuss palms and broad-leaved tropical trees.

Don't miss

The Muséum d'Histoire Naturelle, set behind an 1850s frontage on the edge of the greenery

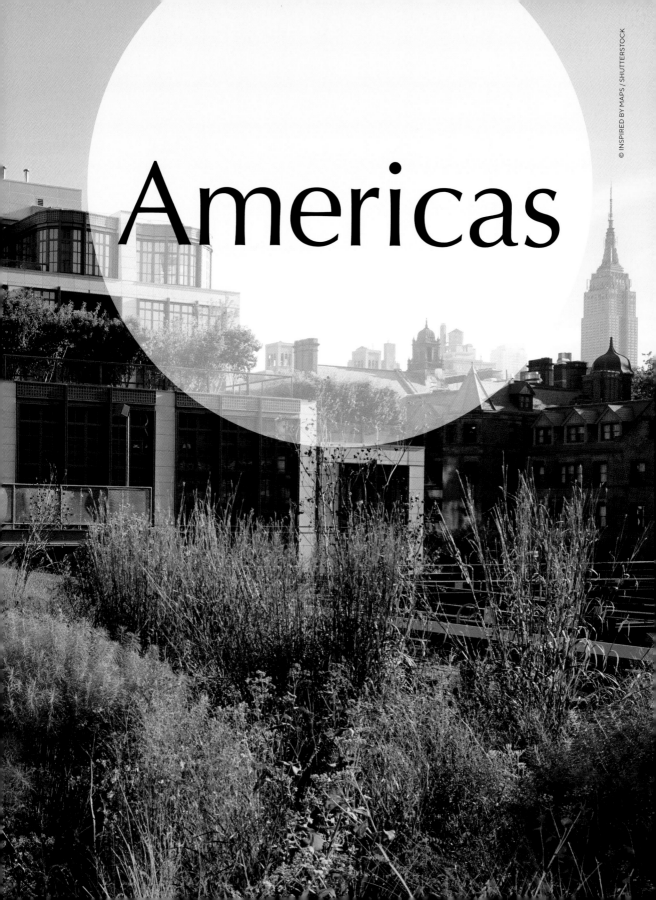

Americas

Linger with live oaks and goddesses

♡ Drama, statuary, festive lights

🕐 December

USA

I t's an arresting vision – an avenue of giant gnarly oak trees draped in feathery Spanish moss. In the distance the statue of a young man wrestles with a wild horse. You could be walking through the pages of a Gothic fairy tale, but this is Brookgreen Gardens, home to the largest collection of American figurative statuary in the US, and a whole lot of Southern magic.

Founded by Archer and Anna Hyatt Huntington in 1931, the 14-sq-mile (36-sq-km) property protects an area of South Carolina's distinctive Lowcountry region of salt marshes, live oaks, longleaf pines, and heritage sites of the Gullah-Geechee people. There are also botanical gardens, art galleries, a historic trail and a Lowcountry Zoo.

Illuminating candlelit festival

Live oaks are native to southeastern USA, where many large and old specimens of the evergreen oaks are found. The majestic Live Oak Allée at Brookgreen Gardens is transformed each December during the Nights of a Thousand Candles, when slender strands of twinkling white lights sway beneath the branches of the 250-year-old trees, casting a haunting glow across the Spanish moss. Throngs of revellers, bundled in their winter coats and snug wool hats, sip warm cider and cluster for photos beneath the stately trees.

It's a scene infused with warmth, goodwill and, thanks to the abundant moss, some ghostly undertones. During the event, the Allée is the centrepiece

Right: Works like *Wind on the Water* by Richard McDermott Miller are staged beautifully

Below: Many of the live oaks were planted in the 1700s; candles add extra sparkle in December

© RICHARD MCDERMOTT MILLER / BROOKGREEN GARDENS

© CRAIG ZERBE / SHUTTERSTOCK

What makes Nights of a Thousand Candles so unique?
You go to a lot of light shows and they kind of look the same, there are Santas and reindeer and all of that. Ours is about taking those live oaks, those 250-year-old trees, and illuminating them in a way – by putting the candles in the garden – that just enhances the structure of what's there.

Santa is overrated anyway. Back to the garden highlights, Brookgreen protects heritage breeds, common here in the 1800s, and native animals. Where can we see them?
At the end of the Lowcountry Trail, we have the heritage breeds. We have Marsh Tacky horses, which are endangered. We have Tunis sheep. We have Spanish goats. On the Lowcountry Trail, in the zoo, are native animals – bald eagles that are non-releasable and red foxes.

Page Kiniry, President & CEO

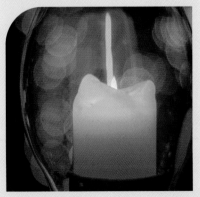

© EPG_EUROPHOTOGRAPHICS / SHUTTERSTOCK

of the gardens, serving as a luminous hub for Brookgreen's vast collection of magnolias, palmettos and lyrical statuary – all enhanced by hand-lit candles and an explosion of colourful lights.

Chasing Diana

Sculpted in 1922 by Anna Hyatt Huntington, the life-size bronze *Diana of the Chase* springs from a garden pool between the entrance and the Live Oak Allée. One of more than 2000 works across the grounds, it became so iconic in its day that Moon Motor Cars reproduced it – in miniature – as a hood ornament for its 'Diana Car' in 1925.

Diana of the Chase is one of seven Diana sculptures in the gardens. Paul Manship's *Diana* dashes from sights unseen, bow drawn, hound at her heels. During Nights of a Thousand Candles she glows an unsettling deep-green against the sky – evoking a concern about whom, exactly, is being chased. It's mesmerising.

Opposite: Enslaved people did much of the landscaping at Middleton Place

Right: Characters from myth and legend, such as *Orpheus* by John Gregory, inhabit the garden

© JOHN GREGORY / BROOKGREEN GARDENS

Walking with the Gullah Geechee

The Lowcountry Trail is an immersive boardwalk journey through longleaf pines and moss-draped live oaks. You'll learn more about the Gullah Geechee people (known as Gullah in South Carolina, Geechee in Georgia), the descendants of enslaved people from West and Central Africa who worked on plantations in the region. The Gullah Geechee preserve a distinct Creole language and culture, and signage and stories on the trail pay tribute to their history.

Don't Miss

→ Scanning for alligators on a boat tour through rice fields

→ Enjoying live music during the Summer Light: Art by Night events

→ Savouring she-crab soup

Find Your Joy

Getting there

The gardens are 18 miles (29km) southwest of Myrtle Beach via US 17. From Charleston, it's an 80-mile (129km) drive.

Accessibility

The gardens are accessible by wheelchair, but Brookgreen does not offer any for rent. Check the website for a list of wheelchair and scooter rental companies. Paved walkways link most gardens and exhibit areas.

When to go

The gardens host Nights of a Thousand Candles Thursday to Sunday evenings in December. Reserve ahead. Azaleas begin to bloom in March and April. Other spring blooms – daffodils, roses, dogwoods – put on a brilliant show through May with magnolias soon to follow.

Further information

• Admission charge.
• Open year-round.
• No dogs allowed.
• Restaurant on-site.
• www.brookgreen.org

Other Southern US Gardens

Middleton Place

Azaleas, live oaks and statuary beg for closer inspection at Middleton Place, overlooking the Ashley River northwest of Charleston. Designed in 1741, they are the oldest landscaped gardens in the US and feature classic formal French gardens, bounded by flooded rice paddies, as well as a woodland garden.

Don't miss

Gaining insight on the Beyond the Fields: Enslavement at Middleton Place tour

Sydney & Walda Besthoff Sculpture Garden

The garden at the New Orleans Museum of Art is home to more than 90 mostly contemporary pieces of sculpture, set among lagoons, live oaks, magnolias and pines. Languid strands of colour, emulating the historic paths of the Mississippi River, snake along the base of the 70ft (21m) *Mississippi Meanders* glass bridge.

Don't miss

The reflective wonders of Jeppe Hein's *Mirror Labyrinth*

Descend into an enchanting flower bowl in Barbados

 Dazzlement, palms, hummingbirds

 December to March

BARBADOS

A former sugar plantation in the agricultural heartland of Barbados might seem like a strange place for a tropical garden, but veteran island horticulturalist Anthony Hunte was never a fan of convention.

Set in a spectacular limestone sinkhole on the grounds of the old Castle Grant Plantation, Hunte's Gardens has converted a land once dominated by a cash crop monoculture into one of the most colourful and biodiverse corners of the island.

The collapsed cave has its own unique microclimate, a fact that Hunte has used to his full advantage to plant a dazzling array of flowers backed by waves of lush greenery that cling to the steep walls.

A natural amphitheatre
As you cross the old weighbridge and enter the gardens, you are greeted by a throng of 120-year-old royal palms with robust grey-white trunks that shoot skywards before exploding outwards in a sea of green fronds like an organic fireworks display. Hovering over the cacophony of colour below, the fronds filter the sunshine, throwing a spotlight on different corners of the gardens throughout the day.

Visitors are given a card of nearly 100 species to try to spot around the garden but keep it in your pocket at first to really take in the vibrant scene, which is enhanced by a classical music soundtrack pumped through unobtrusive speakers by the octogenarian DJ/owner.

From the access way, a number of paths, some stone and others gravel, lead down

Right: Anthony retained a fine collection of royal palms that were already growing on the site

Below: A symphony of colour and texture; showy ginger torch flowers

© SIMON DANNHAUER / SHUTTERSTOCK

© HUNTE'S GARDEN

Q&A

A collapsed cave isn't the easiest of terrains, why did you choose this location?
I've visited gardens all over the world and never seen one in a sinkhole. I knew it would be spectacular!

Does being in a hole pose any particular challenges?
The plants that grow in the sinkhole must be shade lovers; like anthuriums, ferns and palms.

You're famous for your rum-punch, does rum and gardening mix well?
Sugar cane was grown on Castle Grant plantation, so the correlation is quite strong.

The gardens open at 10am, is that too early for punch?
It may be 10am in Barbados, but it's afternoon or midnight in other parts of the world. So, time is just relative!

Anthony Hunte BCH, Proprietor & Horticulturalist

© COREY ANTROBUS / SHUTTERSTOCK

© HUNTE'S GARDEN

Right: Tropical wonderland – the Flower Forest Botanical Gardens

Left: The exuberant result of a lifetime's work and love of tropical horticulture

Don't Miss

→ Sipping a glass of the house rum punch

→ Delighting in the aroma of ginger flowers

→ Seeking out hidden plants on the checklist

into the lower reaches of the garden, decorated all the way with orchids and impatiens that impart bold flourishes of pink, purple and orange.

Hiding behind walls of ferns and handsome bromeliads, stone sculptures and curious antiques emerge from the foliage, making you feel like a treasure hunter exploring a magical tropical world.

Hidden sanctuaries

While the gardens cover just 3 acres (1.2 hectares), the ingenious layout means you can spend an entire morning

or afternoon exploring and still not even scratch the surface. Accessed by short spur paths, a number of hidden mini-gardens set around peaceful water features, overgrown sculptures or spectacular groups of heliconias are found throughout.

Many of these niches have benches and chairs immersed in the vegetation, making them the ideal spot to read a book, enjoy a picnic lunch or just meditate in the lush surrounds. Sitting beside an old copper cauldron encasing delicate water lilies with just butterflies or perhaps a fluttering hummingbird for company, waves of total tranquillity will soon wash over you.

Drinks with the host

At the end of your visit, you can chat with the gregarious Mr Hunte over a drink and a slice of cake, all the while watching brightly plumed birds flit by in the treetops. It's the perfectly genial end to a perfect day.

Find Your Joy

Getting there
Located right in the middle of the island, Hunte's Gardens is on the number 5 bus line from Bridgetown and

is less than an hour's a drive from most accommodation.

Accessibility
A small section of the upper gardens is accessible for wheelchair users, and these areas do provide a fine view of the cascade of plants in the sinkhole. Lower sections are only accessible by a series of steps.

When to go
The gardens are great to visit year-round, but at their very best from December to March when the poinsettias, begonias and kalanchoes are in full bloom.

Further information
• Admission charge.
• Open every day, year-round.
• No dogs allowed.

• Snacks and drinks can be purchased on the balcony of the old stables building.
• www.huntesgardens-barbados.com

Other Barbados Gardens

Andromeda Gardens

Just above the wild Atlantic coast near Bathsheba, these 20-acre (8-hectare) botanical gardens are awash with tropical plants, shrubs and trees. The property is divided by a bubbling stream that forms a series of cascades surrounded by orchids, heliconia, bougainvillea and begonias. A series of winding paths provide the chance to spot colourful bird species, fluttering butterflies and green monkeys.

Don't miss

Browsing the works of talented local artists in the gift shop

Flower Forest Botanical Gardens

Hidden among forest-covered hills in the interior of the island, the 53-acre (22-hectare) Flower Forest Botanical Gardens are home to an immense array of tropical flowers. A circular, wheelchair-friendly path runs through the heart of the gardens past spectacular collections of flowering ginger and banana plants as well as lush bromeliads.

Don't miss

Spotting the locally bred torch ginger: the Flower Forest Heliconia

Learn about First Nations plants, art and culture

♡ Indigenous traditions, rainforest walks, inspiration

🕐 July to September

CANADA

Tofino feels like the edge of the world. Clinging to Vancouver Island's west coast like one of its many surfers gripping their board, this laid-back little town is a long way from British Columbia's mainland. Still, plenty of travellers make the effort to come here to relish this corner of Canadian surfing bliss.

But there's more to tempt than sand and waves. Tofino sits in a coastal rainforest on the traditional territory of the Tla-o-qui-aht First Nation of the Nuu-chah-nulth peoples and the Naa'Waya'Sum Coastal Indigenous Gardens, a conservation scheme run by the Tla-o-qui-aht, highlight the traditional plants and culture of this region, and also offer Indigenous-led activities.

Back to Indigenous lands
Nuu-chah-nulth peoples have lived in western Canada for thousands of years and today members of the community live and work across Vancouver Island, operating hotels, tour companies and other enterprises, including these gardens.

The former Tofino Botanical Gardens opened in 1997, with a mix of old-growth rainforest and cultivated plants. Founder George Patterson owned the waterfront gardens until 2021, when he sold the property to a First Nations-led organisation, the Indigenous Protected and Conserved Areas (IPCA) Innovation Program. The goal of the IPCA is to combine Indigenous knowledge and modern science to promote nature conservation and climate action. In Tofino, the botanical gardens (given their new name in 2022) are

Right: Learn how First Nations people use and conserve the region's many botanical riches

Below: A refreshing and beautiful educational space; a totem pole takes shape

© JEREMY WILLIAMS

© OWEN PERRY

My Garden Joy

The first time I visited these gardens I was surprised to discover this partly wild, partly cultivated corner of the rainforest. I knew that Tofino had beaches and hiking trails, cool cafes and restaurants, and the vast woods and sandy shores of nearby Pacific Rim National Park Reserve. But the gardens were different. Even years before Indigenous guardians took over their management, this was a place that highlighted the First Nations' connection to the land. As I wandered beneath the massive trees, I came upon an artist who was carving a totem pole. He had harvested one of those forest giants to craft a story of his people, a story that I felt privileged to witness taking shape on his traditional lands.

Carolyn B. Heller

© OWEN PERRY

Naa'Waya'Sum Coastal Indigenous Gardens

becoming a hub for Indigenous-led environmental change. A visit here supports this mission and also enables you to learn about the importance of these lands to the local communities.

Learning in the rainforest

Naa'Waya'Sum, the garden's Indigenous name, comes from the traditional Nuu-chah-nulth word for the cedar benches used for sharing knowledge between older and younger generations. As the name suggests, visitors are encouraged to sit in the gardens, breathing in the rainforest air and appreciating the peace and quiet. Trails lead through the woods and along the waterfront beneath the lofty cedars and firs. Small plots feature medicinal and ornamental plants that you can explore as you stroll.

Reinforcing the aim of sharing knowledge, Nuu-chah-nulth carvers are often at work in the gardens. You're welcome to watch them work, ask questions and

Opposite: Poppies blooming at the Tending and Gathering Garden

Right: The Naa'Waya'Sum gardens retain an area of old-growth rainforest

© JEEREMY WILLIAMS

take in the aroma of the freshly carved wood as their creations take shape. Look too for the stone and wood sculptures that artists have crafted and which are placed along the gardens' paths.

Under its new ownership, Naa'Waya'Sum continues to evolve, offering visitors an exciting window into Indigenous culture, heritage and conservation. Walking among the leafy ferns and tall trees, you begin to understand and admire the generations who came before you in this once-remote rainforest along the Pacific coast.

Don't Miss

→ Savouring the fresh rainforest air

→ Watching Indigenous artists as they work

→ Being taught about traditional uses of local medicinal plants

Find Your Joy

Getting there
Naa'Waya'Sum Coastal Indigenous Gardens are 1.5 miles (2.5km) south of Tofino's town centre. A free shuttle, operating late June to early September between town and the Tofino Visitor Centre, stops near the garden. You can also walk or cycle along a paved multi-use path which connects the town, several beaches and Pacific Rim National Park Reserve.

Accessibility
Many areas are not accessible for wheelchairs.

Paths are relatively flat and surfaced with packed gravel or dirt.

When to go
The best time to visit is the drier, sunnier months between May and early October. Book accommodation in advance for July to September, Vancouver Island's peak season. The gardens are closed in winter; check the website to confirm before planning your visit.

Further information
• Admission charge.
• Open March to December.
• Dogs welcome on a lead.
• Cafe on site.
• www.clayoquot campus.ca

More North American Indigenous Gardens

The Tending & Gathering Garden, USA
A partnership between the native Wintun community and the Cache Creek Conservancy, Northern California's Tending and Gathering Garden showcases Indigenous land and plant management practices. From golden lupine to blue elderberry, native plants thrive across the nature preserve.

Don't miss
Learning how *leok po*, (good fire), benefits the local ecosystem

Vesper Meadow, USA
East of the southern Oregon city of Ashland, Vesper Meadow is a project of the Indigenous Gardens Network, which has collaborated with two Southern Oregon groups, the Confederated Tribes of Siletz Indians and the Confederated Tribes of Grand Ronde, to re-establish and manage 'first foods' and other culturally significant plants.

Don't miss
Hearing how certain plants were used by Indigenous communities

© CACHE CREEK CONSERVANCY

Take a stroll in the sky above Manhattan

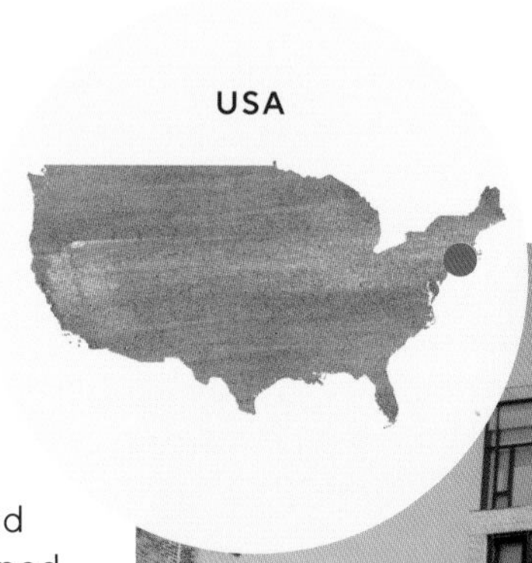

♡ Resilience, city views, native plants

🕐 May

USA

A bumblebee clambers across the domed head of a purple coneflower, its furry legs dusty with pollen. You watch, entranced. The flower sways back and forth under the weight of its visitor, mingling with the surrounding prairie grass. The bee lifts off. You follow it and let your gaze refocus – blue sky, glass and brown brick, epic corridors of buildings. You breathe a deep sigh of contentment. High up and surrounded by plants, you're looking out over the West Side of Manhattan on a spring day.

Raised 30ft (9m) above the traffic below, New York City's High Line gives city-dwellers a much-needed chance to stop and slow down. More than just a green escape, however, this rejuvenated railbed is a testament to community spirit: it was a committed group of locals who campaigned and ultimately saved this abandoned elevated rail line from demolition, refurbishing it for the benefit of both wildlife and urbanites. Opened in 2009, it has been thoughtfully landscaped with native plants and contains multiple different garden zones over its 1.4-mile (2.3km) length. A wander here is uplifting in every sense.

Wild in the city

The project was brought to life by landscape architecture firm James Corner Field Operations, who brought in design studio Diller Scofidio + Renfro and Dutch garden designer Piet Oudolf to oversee the gardens and planting. They took inspiration from the way the abandoned train tracks had become overgrown with self-seeded

Right: From freight to fabulous: the High Line is now one of New York's best loved parks

Below: The High Line gardens were designed to evoke the wild aesthetic of nature

© TIMOTHY SCHENCK / THE HIGH LINE

© MASSIMO SALESI / SHUTTERSTOCK

What is your favourite plant?
I think I'd go with grey birch, *Betula populifolia*. There's a wonderful grove of them at the southern end of the Donald Pels and Wendy Keys Gansevoort Woodland. They're very upright and arch over the path and it's a very evocative experience to walk through them, especially when they're dancing in the wind.

Sounds glorious. What's an unexpected maintenance task?
Many perennials require pinching back beginning in June to ensure they don't get tall and floppy. We have complex plantings and narrow beds, so it's important that each plant holds its space and plays well with its neighbours. Pinching back asters, goldenrods and coreopsis is essential for them to maintain a form that shows off their abundant blooms but still have autumn and winter structural interest.

What's one thing visitors should know?
The naturalistic planting makes everything look deceptively carefree, but the reality is that these are highly maintained gardens requiring skill and dedication to achieve Piet's vision. It's a challenge gardening 30ft (9m) in the air with 18 inches (45cm) of soil, but our 10 horticulturists, assisted by volunteers and seasonal staff, make it look easy.

Richard Hayden, Director of Horticulture

Right: Paris in the spring: the trend-setting Promenade Plantée

Left: At Gansevoort St the garden is planted in tiers creating a cascading effect

Don't Miss

→ Admiring the pre-regeneration High Line at the 16th St Northern Spur Preserve

→ Dipping your toes in the water between 14th and 15th streets

→ Spotting one of 20 species of wild bees

wildflowers, shrubs and grass, and created a design celebrating the region's native species as well as nature's own wild aesthetic. Its 22 zones, planted according to the specific microclimate afforded by each stretch of industrial landscape (wet and windy; sheltered and sunny), are an education in New York's indigenous species. One minute you might be walking through a woodland of shade-tolerant grey birch and serviceberry trees, and the next a meadow of sun-loving perennials. All the while, pollinators and birds flit

about, bringing everything to life. Through the year, new dynamics emerge: leaves turn and fall; flowers become seed heads; and in deepest winter the whole scene turns brown as the plants are left to overwinter naturally, just the vibrant red winterberry standing as a reminder that life goes on.

Urban vibrancy

The magic of the High Line is also found in city elements that predate its creation – the curves and angles of iconic architecture, the brick of old buildings and New Yorkers themselves. Whether it's to jog, stroll or tend the plants as a volunteer, locals and tourists have taken the High Line to their hearts. And while it can become crowded, walking this elevated path lets the rhythms of urban life unfold in all their chaotic beauty, alongside the whisper of wind in the Shenandoah switchgrass and twisted-leaf garlic.

Find Your Joy

Getting there
The High Line runs up the West Side of Manhattan from the Meatpacking District, through Chelsea to 34th St and can be joined at various spots along its route. The A, C, E, L and 7 subway lines come the closest to High Line entry points. Buses, bikes and taxis are all equally good options for getting to it.

Accessibility
The entire High Line is wheelchair accessible, including elevators from street level.

When to go
Warm weekends in spring (April/May) see city denizens come out to sun themselves amid plenty of floral colour; a weekday or slightly grim weather means smaller crowds. The native plantings have interest in all seasons.

Further information
• Free admission.
• Open daily; hours change seasonally.
• No dogs allowed.
• Some pop-up dining.
• www.thehighline.org

Other Elevated Urban Gardens

La Promenade Plantée, France

The original repurposed rail-line-turned-public-park is still going strong. The route covers three miles (5km) from Paris' Place de la Bastille to Bois de Vincennes along a defunct viaduct which was transformed in 1993, inspiring Parisians and cities across the world in one fell swoop. Only 33ft (10m) wide, it is thick with lavender, wisteria, roses, lime trees and other enticing plants.

Don't miss
Traversing the suspended walkway above Jardin de Reuilly

Seoullo 7017, South Korea

Once a highway overpass, now a garden, Seoullo 7017 transformed at lightning speed to become an elevated open walkway of plants, within and yet not quite part of South Korea's capital. It's an educational arboretum filled with native trees, offering a respite from the busy city and a great vantage point for urban views.

Don't miss
Taking an evening stroll when the garden is lit up in blue

Explore Colombia's biodiversity in one urban garden

COLOMBIA

♡ Water features, amazement, views

🕐 December to February

The largest botanical garden in Colombia is not only a serene escape from its capital city's hectic streets but also a journey around the country through its plants, trees and medicinal herbs. Illustrating the biodiversity of this relatively compact nation, from the mountains of the Andes and the Sierra Nevada to the tropical Caribbean coast, the garden showcases a wonderful array of plants, from pines, palms and plantains to a significant collection of roughly 4000 species of orchids. The rich diversity conserved here inspires hope for our planet's ecological future.

Gardens under glass
The signature exhibition area is the futuristic Tropicario, the largest greenhouse in South America, encompassing six glass domes – one reserved for changing exhibitions, the others recreating specific botanical environments found across the country.

Wander into the humid jungle-like Bosque Húmedo Tropical, a rainforest where, even though you're indoors, you'll feel like you're walking beneath a misty green canopy. Compare these lush surroundings with the Bosque Seco Tropical (tropical dry forest), where cacti, succulents and other desert plants predominate, or to the rocky Superpáramo, a high-altitude region found above 13,000ft (3960m). The large-format photographs that line the walls here immerse you in this area of snow-topped peaks and hardy vegetation.

Right: The six greenhouses are climatised to varying degrees of warmth and humidity

Below: The garden has a focus on High Andean plants; a garden of science and beauty

Q&A

Why do you bring international students to Bogotá's botanical garden? It's not only for the plants, is it?
No, it's not. Along with the immense range of vegetation on display, the garden also recalls the time in our history when José Celestino Mutis led the great expedition that discovered just how environmentally varied Colombia is.

And besides history?
This is also a place to do birdwatching and to discover beautiful butterflies and insects. It's a complete cultural, biodiversity and community experience.

What are your favourite areas of the garden?
The Tropicario, which represents Colombia's various ecosystems, La Maloca and its displays on the Indigenous culture of the Amazon, and the medicinal plants zone are of particular interest to me.

Rafael Mauricio Fonseca Montañez, Coordinator of Cultural Activities, Nueva Lengua Spanish School

Another section is devoted to orchids and bromeliads – enjoy their dramatic blooms and snap close-up photographs of their intriguing shapes and colours.

Roses, palms and some history

The botanical garden also has several outdoor areas to explore. Smell the blossoms in La Rosaleda (the rose garden) and feel the breeze beneath tall, slender palm trees that stretch toward the clouds. As you wander the paths, you'll find ferns and flowers, a herb garden and a wide variety of trees that shade you from both the sun and the city's frequent rain showers.

The gardens take their name from the 18th-century Spanish botanist José Celestino Mutis, who led the Royal Botanical Expedition of the Kingdom of New Granada across what is now Colombia in the late 1700s and early 1800s. Although the biodiversity he encountered would have been well-known to

Opposite: Around 60% of Rio's botanical garden is natural Atlantic forest

Right: The garden preserves flowers from the Amazon, and has many different species of palm

© JARDÍN BOTÁNICO DE BOGOTÁ JOSÉ CELESTINO MUTIS

its Indigenous peoples, Mutis was the first to document this natural richness for the wider world, and the garden continues to be an important centre of research into the country's ecosystems today.

See if you can locate the Mutisia clematis, the climbing, flowering vine named in his honour. Also look for the large, thatch-roofed La Maloca, with exhibits on Indigenous culture. There are lakes and waterfalls, fruit trees and aquatic plants, too, so pace yourself as you travel across Colombia, one plant at a time.

Don't Miss

➡ **Breathing the Tropicario's steamy air**

➡ **Craning to admire palm trees that seem to touch the sky**

➡ **Choosing your favourite scent from the many roses**

Find Your Joy

Getting there

You can reach the botanical garden by bus from many points around the city, although in sprawling Bogotá it may be faster to travel by ride share or taxi. The gardens are 5 miles (8km) southeast of the airport and 7 miles (11 km) northwest of historic La Candelaria neighbourhood.

Accessibility

Most of the garden's exterior paths are paved or made from cobblestone, making them bumpy but navigable for people with mobility issues including wheelchair users. Ramps take you through the Tropicario's greenhouses.

When to go

While Bogotá's climate is temperate year-round, consider avoiding the rainier months of April, May, October and November, though really you can visit the gardens at any time as the greenhouses protect you from the weather. Come in December to view the twinkling holiday lights.

Further information
• Admission charge.
• Open year-round.
• No dogs allowed.
• Cafe on site.
• https://jbb.gov.co

More South American Botanical Gardens

Jardim Botânico do Rio de Janeiro, Brazil

More than 8000 plant species in this historical space lure visitors away from Rio's beaches. Designed in 1808, the garden includes cacti, medicinal plants and thousands of bromeliads. Wander the walkways lined with 100ft (30m) palms, then admire the Vitória Régia, considered the largest of the world's water lilies.

Don't miss

Marvelling at 600 species of orchids in the fragrant *orquidário*

Jardín Botánico de Quito, Ecuador

Ramble through cloud forest, Andean *páramo* (high-elevation grasslands), wetlands and more as you discover Ecuador's major ecosystems in this garden in the country's capital, Quito. Check out the bonsai exhibits, the roses and, especially, the diverse collection of palms.

Don't miss

Learning about the plants that the region's Indigenous peoples incorporate into their daily lives

Commune with death – and life – at Mt Auburn

♡ History, trees, contemplation

🕐 September and October

To stand on a hill beneath the orange-leaved oak trees of Mt Auburn Cemetery is to understand what the 19th-century Romantic poets were talking about. Life is transient, beauty ephemeral, sadness and joy exist side-by-side.

Making death beautiful

Mt Auburn is a garden and an arboretum, but it's also the final resting place of nearly 100,000 people. Opened in 1831, it was the first of America's so-called 'garden cemeteries'. Before Mt Auburn, the dead were buried in crowded, increasingly unsanitary churchyards. Two leading Bostonians, a doctor and a Harvard botany professor, proposed a solution – a rural cemetery where graves could exist alongside trees and shrubs. It would solve the crowding problem and make death seem more natural, less frightening.

It's impossible to stroll the wooded paths without contemplating mortality. There are trees – white oaks and beeches, gingkos and weeping willows, maples and bristlecone pines – that were here before our grandparents were born and will be here after our own grandchildren are gone. The graves and mausoleums and memorial towers honour people who were as real as we are, now turned to dust.

But Mt Auburn is hardly a gloomy place. In spring, the air is perfumed with the scent of roses, lilacs, azaleas, wisteria, honeysuckle and tree peonies. In summer, the chapels host string

USA

Right: Climb the 62ft (19m) Washington Tower for a bird's eye view of the cemetery

Below: Designed as a more elegant resting place, Mt Auburn was inspired by Père Lachaise

Q&A

What would you recommend a first-time visitor to Mt Auburn be sure to do?
Go up to Bigelow Chapel lawn and see the Sphinx Civil War Memorial. Then I think it's just incredible to climb the Washington Tower – it gives you a sense of Boston; you can see the State House, the Zakim Bridge, the Bunker Hill Monument, Wachusett Mountain.

Done. Sounds awesome. What feelings does the cemetery evoke for you?
It's a place where it's OK to be melancholic. It's a place where it's OK to be grieving. And it's also OK to be birding. It's a place where you really are able to feel healed by nature.

It is certainly a soothing place. Do you have any favourite grave inscriptions?
Everyone loves the one that says 'She Hath Done What She Could.'

Do you have any other advice for visitors?
Plan to get lost! Just wander.

Meg L. Winslow, Curator of Historical Collections & Archives

Right: John Muir once spent six days and nights in Bonaventure Cemetery

Left: Bigelow Chapel was designed by one of the cemeteries founders, Jacob Bigelow

Chapel strike a note of drama, while English country-style Story Chapel is a gentler counterpoint. Both are excellent spots to contemplate the sublime.

Further inside, the miles of paths, winding through lawns, gardens and woodland, bring moments of reflection and flashes of surprising levity. Your heart aches to see a tiny stone bassinet memorialising a lost baby. You feel a renewed faith in love upon reading a romantic letter inscribed on a grave marker. You laugh at the quote on a 19th-century clown's headstone.

Wander long enough and you'll find Consecration Dell, a wooded valley at the cemetery's heart. Restored in the 1990s, it's most like the Mt Auburn of nearly 200 years ago. The dell vibrates at a slightly different frequency. It's warmer in winter, cooler in summer. It's quieter too. It's hard to stand within its leafy embrace and not feel a sense of renewal, even rebirth.

Don't Miss

→ **Meditating by the burbling fountain in the Asa Gray Garden**

→ **Beholding Boston from the Washington Tower**

→ **Seeking out the graves of famous poets and other luminaries**

quartets and artist residencies. In autumn, wild turkeys waddle across the footpaths. In winter, children in snowsuits shriek at the thrill of fresh drifts.

From sadness to laughter

A single visit can take you through a range of emotions. The new Asa Gray Garden serves as a peaceful link between the cemetery and the outside world. It has some 170 species of East Asian and Eastern US plants, commemorating the work of pioneering botanist Asa Gray. Beyond, the spires and stained glass of Bigelow

Find Your Joy

Getting there

From Harvard Square it's a 30-minute walk or a 10-minute car or bus trip. From downtown Boston, it's a 20-minute drive or

a combo of the Red Line T (underground rail) and the bus.

Accessibility

Both chapels are wheelchair accessible, and there are two major paved paths circling the grounds. Smaller woodland trails weaving through graves are unpaved, uneven and can be steep.

When to go

April and May bring a profusion of blooms, while September and October mean classic New England fall colours. A December winter solstice event with light installations often sells out in advance.

Further information

• Free admission.
• Open year-round.
• No dogs allowed.
• No cafe or restaurant.
• www.mount auburn.org

Other Garden Cemeteries

Bonaventure Cemetery, USA

Dripping with Spanish moss and scented with azaleas, Bonaventure, in Savannah, defines Southern Gothic. Marble cherubs, weeping maiden statues and ornate mausoleums are set among ancient trees, including a striking avenue of live oaks. Wander ferny dells, lose yourself in overgrown palmetto groves, and sit on sun-dappled hillocks overlooking the Wilmington River.

Don't miss

Bringing a flower to little Gracie Watson's statue

Père Lachaise Cemetery, France

Considered the world's first garden cemetery, Paris' Père Lachaise was originally such a hike from town it attracted few visitors and even fewer burials. Today, the huge necropolis is firmly on the list of Parisian must-sees. Famous residents include Frédéric Chopin, Edith Piaf and Oscar Wilde. Lanes are planted with maple and ash trees, rose gardens and blooming hedges.

Don't miss

Following the graffiti arrows to Jim Morrison's grave

Embrace the beauty of the desert – but carefully!

♡ Cacti and succulents, tranquillity, wildflowers

🕐 March and April

USA

Three glassworks by Dale Chihuly soar skyward at the entrance to the Desert Botanical Garden in Phoenix, Arizona. Dubbed *Desert Towers*, this permanent art installation tucked among tidy rows of agave and barrel cacti has a fiery green exuberance that's a mischievous wink – a suggestion that your expectations about desert flora are about to be upended.

A fuzzy welcome

The mischief emerges early on the Sonoran Desert Nature Loop, one of five themed trails meandering across the 55 acres (22 hectares) of cultivated gardens. As you walk, the scene starts to resemble the wildest party in town: the arms of the barrel-chested saguaros are lifted in welcome, the tiny teddy bear chollas are a furry explosion of fun, the reedy ocotillos are doing their own dance, the prickly pears are up to no good and the handful of elegant organ pipe cacti? Well, they're actually at the wrong party, but they're always game for a good time – as long as they don't get too cold.

Beyond their elegance, some of the organ pipes here do have an inspiring story to tell. Two of them are 'rescue cacti', having been saved from destructive mining activities in other parts of the state – one in 1940 and the other in 1980. Thanks to the garden's day-one mission to protect desert flora, they've been thriving ever since.

Wildflowers and butterflies

Another surreal touch? The cactus blooms, which begin

Right: Agave and other desert denizens growing among the glass strands of an art installation

Below: A prickly party awaits – the garden fosters appreciation of desert ecosystems; a monarch butterfly

Q&A

What do you love about the gardens?
The desert flora is spectacularly unique.

Can we chat cacti. Cardons are the world's largest cactus and they're right here!
The cardons that we have on display, the largest ones, date back to the founding of the gardens [in 1939]. We have photos from way back in the day, they were maybe 5ft (1.5m) tall and now you have to crane your neck to look up and see the top.

One of many cacti occupational hazards. Do you have a favourite spring bloom?
The prickly pears. We sometimes call them the rose of the desert when they're blooming. The blooms are, depending on the species, all kinds of colours. And they're very lush, like roses.

Kimberlie McCue, Chief Science Officer

to appear along the Desert Wildflower Loop in mid-February. Whether it's a lone white flower atop a saguaro or the technicolor blossoms of a prickly pear, it's easy to assign metaphorical importance to these eye-catching wonders: they're harbingers of hope. A salve for mental wounds. Or bright fists punching against life's existential monotony.

Photographers will long remember the challenge of trying to photograph one of the 2000 butterflies fluttering through the Butterfly Pavilion. Awash in bright colours but extremely fidgety, these delicate and ephemeral pollinators rarely sit still for a close-up.

Art in the garden

Every year from October to the end of May the garden showcases the art of one major artist who installs creative works across the grounds. From the ebullient glasswork of Chihuly

Opposite: The Boyce Thompson Arboretum attracts migratory birds

Right: Desert flowers, such as this desert rose, are often vivid in colour

© SATHIT HUAYSAN / SHUTTERSTOCK

to the sensual sculptures of Rotraut, past installations have varied wildly. Never boring, they complement – and sometimes disrupt – the stark grandeur of the desert. But whatever the goal, the installations all add one thing: aesthetic oomph that elevates the scene, bringing a little razzle-dazzle to rust-coloured buttes, scrubby mountains and swathes of succulent greenery. Nevertheless, the artistry of Mother Nature at sunset, when the red hills turn luminous and the bright blooms reflect the dying light, is unrivaled.

Don't Miss

➞ Watching hummingbirds zip between wildflowers

➞ Admiring the golden-hour glow illuminating saguaros and red rocks

➞ Consuming doughnut holes with prickly pear sauce

Find Your Joy

Getting there
From downtown Phoenix take the light rail east to Priest Dr/Washington St then walk around the corner to Priest Dr

to catch Bus 36 to the garden. It'll take about an hour. From downtown it's a 15-minute drive.

Accessibility
The garden trails are fully accessible to wheelchairs, and strollers will be fine on most of them. Wheelchairs and scooters can be rented at the admissions office on a first-come, first-served basis.

When to go
For wildflower and cactus blooms, the best time to visit is February to the end of April. Luminaries and holiday lights brighten the gardens Thursday to Sundays nights in December. Reservations are required. From June to much of September it's scorchingly hot.

Further information
• Admission charge.
• Open year-round.
• No dogs allowed, except service dogs.
• Restaurant on-site.
• www.dbg.org

Other US Desert Gardens

Arizona-Sonora Desert Museum

One part botanical garden, one part zoo and one part museum, this 98-acre (40-hectare) ode to the Sonoran Desert is a highlight of any visit to Tucson, Arizona. Desert dwellers (coatis, prairie dogs, javelina) grab the spotlight but the museum is also home to 12,000 types of plants. Spot many of them while strolling the Desert Grassland exhibit and the Desert Loop Trail.

Don't miss

The Packrat Playhouse, if travelling with kids

Boyce Thompson Arboretum

This much-loved arboretum 60 miles (96.5km) southeast of Phoenix in Superior, Arizona celebrates the adaptability and variety of plant life. Thousands of arid-country trees and plants from around the world are spread across 135 acres (57 hectares) of gardens.

Don't miss

Taking a walk through the 13-acre (5-hectare) Wallace Desert Garden

© LUCIA W / SHUTTERSTOCK

Lose yourself in a surrealist jungle garden

♡ Sculpture, jungle, daydreaming

🕐 February

MEXICO

A winding staircase juts skyward in a spiral, mossy columns are crowned by flowering epiphytes and a pair of concrete hands rises out of the ground like a ghostly apparition. Even in your wildest dreams it would be hard to envisage a garden as ambitious and fanciful as Las Pozas.

Comprising a collection of concrete sculptures embedded in the jungle in eastern Mexico, the project sprang from the imagination of late British poet Edward James who came to the region in the 1940s. James, a patron of surrealist art, wanted to create his own Garden of Eden in one of the country's remotest corners. Armed with a weighty inheritance and over 80 acres (32 hectares) of land adapted from a coffee plantation, he came tantalisingly close.

Concrete as art

Situated on the slopes of the Sierra Madre Oriental, Las Pozas acquired its current layout in the early 1960s after a freak winter storm killed James' prized orchid collection. Seeking to establish something more lasting and weather resistant, he redesigned his garden around a necklace of natural pools (*pozas* in Spanish) and waterfalls and punctuated it with whimsical temples, pagodas, bridges, pavilions and spiral stairways made from reinforced concrete. Reflecting his love of surrealism, the structures were purely aesthetic. Paved paths wind past giant concrete mushrooms, staircases appear suspended in mid-air and buildings with bizarre names like 'the house with three floors that might be five' look like something out of a Salvador Dalí painting.

Right: Many of the sculptures have plant-like shapes and were intended to blend with nature

Below: Some of the structures were made to house James's exotic pets; a surrealist greeting

Q&A

What's your favourite sculpture?
Without doubt, the Palace of Bamboo. It's simply magical, its concrete bamboo rising in the middle of the jungle. If you are one of the privileged people to visit on the private 'El Edén en el Jardín' tour you can climb to the third floor and have the sensation of admiring Las Pozas like a bird visiting the forgotten garden of an ancient civilisation.

How many orchid species are there?
We have recorded 22 species in the garden.

What's your favourite time of year?
February. It's a time with only a small influx of visitors so you can enjoy the garden better, hearing the waterfalls and the chirping of birds while the sculptures are hidden in seasonal mist.

Joe Richaud, Public Relations Manager

© GOOGLE ARTS & CULTURE / JARDÍN ESCULTÓRICO EDWARD JAMES

An unusual harmony

On paper, the project sounds like a massive folly, yet in reality the combination of luxuriant jungle and other-worldly art is strangely harmonious. Navigating the labyrinthine walkways, amid overhanging ferns and turquoise pools, evokes a sense of dream-like wonder. It's almost like you've entered the pages of a magic realism novel or stumbled upon the overgrown ruins of a lost pre-Columbian city.

Enter the labyrinth

You're welcomed to the garden by the Cinematógrafo, an outlandish multi-storey structure with an unfinished top floor. Exposed steps twist around columns shaped like champagne glasses. A trail beyond leads through a ring-shaped doorway and past sculpted serpents to the arches and pillars of the so-called Parrot House. Deeper inside the maze, the Palace of Bamboo juxtaposes concrete

Opposite: The bench in Parc Güell was shaped around a worker's bare bottom

Right: The forest at Las Pozas is full of natural springs and magical scenery

bamboo with the real thing, while nearby the 'house with a roof like a whale' and the 'bathtub shaped like an eye' leave you wondering if you imbibed something hallucinogenic with your morning coffee.

The garden's final flourish, the Temple of the Ducks, sits in front of a plunging waterfall and crystal-clear pool. Here, you can relax amid rustling foliage and fluttering butterflies and marvel at the audacity of James' vision, a horticultural masterwork fuelled by his rich and fertile surrealistic fantasies.

Don't Miss

➜ Strolling past bird of paradise buttresses and concrete mushrooms

➜ Crossing the *puente* (bridge) lined with fleur-de-lis motifs

➜ Admiring the vegetal forms of the *Cornucopia* sculpture

Find Your Joy

Getting there

The garden is in Xilitla which is a 4½-hour drive from San Luis Potosí and its international airport. If coming by bus, you'll need

to change in Ciudad Valles (total journey time: six hours). From Mexico City it's an eight-hour car drive, or around 10-12 hours on a bus (with changes).

Accessibility

With its steep winding paths, narrow passageways and copious steps, the garden is not suitable for people with limited mobility.

When to go

To avoid crowds, come in the quieter months, namely January, February, September and October. Mondays and Wednesdays are invariably the least busy days of the week. It's usually drier and cooler in the winter (December to March).

Further information

• Admission charge. Booking online in advance recommended.
• Open year-round.
• No dogs allowed.
• No restaurant. No food permitted in the garden.
• https://laspozas xilitla.org.mx

Other Surrealist Gardens

Park Güell, Spain
Barcelona's Park Güell is where art nouveau architect Antoni Gaudí turned his hand to landscape gardening. The result is an enchanting urban park guarded by two Hansel-and-Gretel gatehouses. Curvaceous buildings and multi-coloured mosaics complement the natural setting (oaks, pines, wisteria, olive trees and magnolias), and city views.

Don't miss
Following the wonderful Banc de Trencadís, a tiled, curving bench

Europos Parkas, Lithuania
Located at the geographical centre of Europe, this sculpture park is set amid 136 acres (55 hectares) of undulating grass and woodland. The complex is home to over 100 outdoor artworks created by international artists. Together they blend perfectly with the rustling trees and flower-studded meadows.

Don't miss
Counting 3000 television sets in the *LNK Infotree*, allegedly the world's largest sculpture

© BOULE13 / GETTY IMAGES

Be dazzled by seasonal variety at these historic gardens

♡ Wonderment, local heritage, refreshing rainforests

🕐 July and August

CANADA

These manicured gardens on Vancouver Island, near British Columbia's capital Victoria, are gorgeous in every season, from their springtime cherry trees to their holiday lights. And behind the botanical beauty, there's an interesting history, too. It was one Jennie Butchart's vision that transformed her and her husband Robert's stone quarry and cement factory – and their large estate overlooking the Saanich Inlet – into the region's most beloved and vibrant garden.

A welcoming place
In 1904, the Butcharts moved to Vancouver Island to construct a cement plant using the area's limestone deposits. They built their home, dubbed 'Benvenuto' (Italian for 'Welcome'), on the grounds, and Jennie began working with a Japanese landscape architect to design a Japanese-style garden above the waterfront.

By 1909, when the limestone had been depleted, Jennie set to work creating a garden in its place, filling in the quarry to develop what became the Sunken Garden. Taking nine years to complete, this section now comprises 150 flower beds with a 70ft (21m) fountain at one end. From the lookout point you can survey the expanse of blossoming trees and beds of annuals, and be awed by Jennie's grand garden vision.

The Butcharts continued expanding their creation, converting a tennis court into the Italian Garden where today you can rest over a creamy gelato. They planted the 2500 individual

Right: Jennie Butchart was untrained in horticulture but had an artist's eye for colour

Below: The Sunken Garden's spring explosion of tulips; a Himalayan blue poppy

Q&A

What are the gardens' most unusual plants?
Our most famous flower is the Himalayan blue poppy. We also have our own orchid, 'Benvenuto'.

What might people not know about the gardens?
The Butchart Gardens are very environmentally proactive. To protect the natural surroundings, drought-tolerant trees such as giant sequoia, lodgepole pine and leyland cypress have been planted in our forested areas. And we use recycled water from our own reservoirs.

Do you have a favourite time to visit?
I'd say early morning during springtime when the flowers emerge. I'm also fond of spending summer evenings along the perennial borders and autumn afternoons amongst the falling leaves. And even in winter the garden is magical as the sun sets over the hills.

Thea Hegland, Supervisor, Gardening Department

© SHAWN TALBOT / SHUTTERSTOCK

Right: Keukenhof was established in 1949 to flaunt the produce of local bulb growers

Left: Step into the tranquil Japanese Garden with its flowing streams and 74 maple trees

Don't Miss

→ **Wandering beneath the pink cherry blossoms in spring**

→ **Sipping afternoon tea among the flowers**

→ **Oohing and aahing at the fireworks illuminating the summer skies**

rose plants, representing 280 different varieties, which fill the Rose Garden. In July and August, when the roses are in full bloom, wander beneath the fragrant flowering archways to revel in their aromatic bouquet.

The gardens' exotic plants and curated grounds give it a formal feel, yet among the greenery and trees there are reminders that you're also exploring a coastal rainforest. Stop to breathe in the fresh air on the paths where Jennie herself planted many of the trees that still shade the space today.

Honouring heritage

Wandering the flower-lined paths here transports you back to a time when garden beds were carefully manicured and strolling amid the blossoms was a decorous diversion, perhaps with dresses swishing beneath a parasol or a fedora deflecting the afternoon sun. You can recall those days with a traditional high tea, served in the Butcharts' former house.

But while European gardens inspired their design, the Butchart Gardens are on the traditional land of the W̱SÁNEĆ Nation and acknowledge their Indigenous heritage too. Look for the two totem poles that local First Nations master carvers crafted onsite for the gardens' centenary celebrations.

Although Jennie passed away in 1950 and Robert in 1943, the family legacy and the gardens live on with their great-granddaughter, Robin-Lee Clarke, the Butchart's current owner.

Find Your Joy

Getting there

From downtown Victoria, BC Transit buses travel to the gardens in under an hour. If you've arrived from the mainland at BC Ferries' Swartz Bay Terminal, you can catch a BC Transit bus directly here.

Accessibility

Most of the garden paths are accessible to people with mobility issues. Where pathways are too steep or narrow for wheelchair access, signage and garden maps suggest alternative routes.

When to go

Visit in April and May when blossoming cherries, magnolias and more than 300 varieties of rhododendron signal the end of winter. June through August brings roses, hydrangeas and begonias, along with dramatic weekend fireworks displays. By October, autumn colours are in full view. During the December holidays thousands of lights sparkle along the garden paths.

Further information
• Admission charge.
• Open year-round.
• Dogs welcome.
• Restaurant and cafe on site.
• www.butchart gardens.com

Other Flower-Display Gardens

Longwood Gardens, USA

Like the Butchart Gardens, Pennsylvania's Longwood Gardens were originally developed in the early 1900s from one individual's vision. Pierre du Pont modelled these gardens on several of Europe's grandest expanses of flowers and greenery. More than 11,000 types of plants grow across its 1050 acres (425 hectares).

Don't miss

Finding your way through the maze in the Children's Garden

Keukenhof, The Netherlands

Plan ahead to see the world's largest bulb-flower garden with its more than seven million blooms. Located in Lisse, 25 miles (40km) southwest of Amsterdam, the Keukenhof is open for only eight weeks every year, between mid-March and mid-May. The garden season begins when crocuses and daffodils peek above the earth and hyacinths start to blossom.

Don't miss

Trying to photograph the 800 multicoloured varieties of tulips

Connect with nature in a preserved Mexican paradise

 Calm, cacti, spirituality

 June and July

MEXICO

Flashes of red, a Vermilion flycatcher, dance across the branches of a mesquite tree. The orange specks of a Monarch butterfly burst on white izote flowers. Silhouettes of *Pachycereus marginatus* cacti stand like sentinels, surveying the garden and the large water reservoir behind. To the west, a ravine drops over a dam wall and disappears into the distance. To the east, trails wind through a desert nirvana of long, yellow-brown grasses, more cacti and lime-coloured succulents, interspersed with lookouts and rest points. Welcome to El Charco del Ingenio, one of the world's most extraordinary, rehabilitated gardens.

In the 1980s, this was the last of seven canyons in the Laja River watershed that had not been consumed by San Miguel de Allende's encroaching suburbia. A group of concerned locals devised a plan – purchase the canyon and save its endangered semi-desert flora. The result? A conservation area and enthnobotanic garden with over 600 plant species (in 1991, it was just 131), all the result of natural regeneration. And that's not counting 450 Mexican succulents and cacti.

But El Charco extends beyond mere inventory. Entering here is like walking into a meditation zone where you're enveloped by silence, broken only by the intermittent sounds of birds and wind.

Cultural and spiritual revival
There's a sense of spirituality too at the Four Winds Plaza lookout which you feel

Right: The main pavilion displays just a sample of the garden's botanical collection

Below: Trails invite discovery; the garden was named a 'Peace Zone' by the Dalai Lama

© EL CHARCO DEL INGENIO

© EL CHARCO DEL INGENIO

Q&A

Many people have an aversion to cacti. What would you say to them?
Yes, true. Probably because cacti have thorns! These were once leaves. Every plant has different strategies to survive and cacti have their thorns.

But do you think that explanation will convert sceptics?
You're not marrying a cactus! Plus, other lovely plants grow in El Charco too: trees, succulents, and over 37 varieties of ferns.

True. So what do you hope people experience when they visit?
An appreciation of the desert and semi-desert plants from around Mexico and around the world we have here. And don't forget the flowers – they are amazing as well.

Yes, they are indeed spectacular. So should a visitor approach the garden clockwise or anti-clockwise?
Just go wherever the energy pulls you.

César Arias, Co-creator

© EL CHARCO DEL INGENIO

immediately. Perhaps it's because this space commemorates the 1991 solar eclipse when Indigenous communities gathered for the Fiesta de la Santa Cruz del Charco del Ingenio. Or because you're standing on the spot where their ancestors once gathered these plants for use in their daily lives.

Opposite: Spiny splendour: the Jardín Etnobotánico de Oaxaca

Right: The garden preserves over 500 cacti species, from squat and spiky to tall and hairy

© EL CHARCO DEL INGENIO

Go with the flow
The Conservatory of Mexican Plants feels like a sacred refuge. Protecting species from around the country, it's a warm, peaceful and mesmerising experience.

Elsewhere, the garden invites fluid discovery of the meandering kind. Plants separate the collections and zones, and unearthing these areas casually – the interactive Garden of the Senses; the Sculpture Trail's partially concealed carvings and statues; the spiral-shaped amphitheatre-sundial that indicates the equinoxes and solstices – is part of the magic.

Lasting legacies and legends
On the verge of the wetlands are historic vestiges: a former 16th-century water mill; a dam wall; an aqueduct. And omnipresent, in the hum of the insects and the touch of the breeze, is the aura of El Chan. For millennia, this mythical, underworld creature is said to have lived in the canyon's pond, guarding San Miguel's only remaining spring. Given the recent discovery of a new plant species in El Charco, *Peperomia tancitaroana*, it seems that El Chan wields its supernatural power beyond the water.

Don't Miss
→ Communing with El Chan in the gorge

→ Birdwatching along the canyon trails

→ Learning lots in the Conservatory of Mexican Plants

Find Your Joy

Getting there
Take a taxi from San Miguel. To return, a wonderful downhill walk with fabulous views takes you through an outer suburb before ending back in town.

Accessibility
While paths are defined, they comprise loose gravel. Adventurous wheelchair users can access the main trails, but not venture into the gorge. The ethnobotanical garden with aromatic plants and the pollinators' garden that attracts insects and birds provide sensory experiences.

When to go
Any time of year is wonderful. Every season sees birdlife; rainy season (especially June and July) brings lush green vegetation and flowers; the annual Fiesta de la Santa Cruz del Charco del Ingenio is in the second week of July.

Further information
• Admission charge.
• Open year-round.
• No dogs allowed.
• An excellent cafe serves salads and a daily Mexican special.
• www.elcharco.org.mx

Other Mexican Ethnobotanical Gardens

Jardín Etnobotánico de Oaxaca

Originally part of the Santo Domingo monastery grounds, the Jardín Etnobotanico de Oaxaca has a similar history to El Charco. With the prospect of a luxury hotel on the site, locals fought the state government, and won. These days, the garden displays an astonishing range of plant species that are native to Oaxaca state.

Don't miss
Catching the light in the reflecting pool

Jardín Etnobotánico del Centro INAH Morelos

This Cuernavaca-located garden forms part of the Antigua Villa del Olindo, a summer residence commissioned by Maximilian of Habsburg in 1866. The garden conserves ethnobotanical wisdom of both rural and Indigenous populations, and holds Mexico's largest collection of medicinal plants.

Don't miss
Exploring the herbarium and orchid collection

Marvel at themed gardens and historical collections

♡ Palms, variety, inspiration

◷ February and March

Wend your way through the peaceful Japanese Garden pausing to inspect bonsai trees and *suiseki* (viewing) stones. Then pass beneath the fronds of 90 different species of palm, gathered from the world's arid and subtropical regions. Next up is the prickly Desert Garden, one of the oldest and largest collections of cacti on the planet. Whichever way you turn, your heart leaps as intriguing flora peep out.

Set out over 130 acres (53 hectares), the Huntington's 16 extraordinary themed gardens, developed over a century of determined horticulture, transport visitors across different climes. Taken together, its diversity makes any garden-lover giddy. Pick a handful of themes for a slow day of discovery, and vow to return.

An illustrious history

The Huntington was formally founded in 1919 by Arabella Huntington and her third husband, rail magnate and real estate tycoon Henry E Huntington. The couple had enormous combined wealth and were avid collectors of art, rare books and, especially Henry, plants. The grounds of their ranch in balmy Southern California evolved over the years from simple orchards to formidable collections of orchids, cacti and rare and unusual species sourced from all over the world.

To roam the gardens now is to experience microclimates

Right: Splash zones, fairy doors and whirlygig topiaries delight in the Children's Garden

Below: Trendy for its time, the Japanese Garden was completed in 1912; the Desert Garden

© NOAH SAUVE / SHUTTERSTOCK

© ANUP CHAUHAN / 500PX

Q&A

Do you have a favourite plant collection on site?
Like parents with their children, we try not to have favourites. But the most popular gardens and collections with the public are the Rose Garden, Japanese Garden, Chinese Garden and Desert Garden.

Which garden represents the biggest challenge?
The Desert Garden and Desert Collection, which include 60% of the 27,000 plant taxa here. Much skill and attention are needed to keep track of these many small plants in the records database and on the map.

How do garden staff protect plantings against extreme heat or cold?
We have greenhouses for tropical collections like orchids, arums and bromeliads that need extra protection from the cold. Other than that, we don't do anything special. In fact, we have a long history of testing plant adaptions here.

Nicole Cavender, Director of the Botanical Gardens

© NOAH SAUVE / SHUTTERSTOCK

that have been developed over a century and continue expanding. A Canary Island date palm was one of the earliest additions and can still be found on the grounds. The newest section is the Chinese Garden, the largest outside China, its pavilions linked by picturesque bridges. Wander the paths and be awed by the vision of the Huntingtons and the landscape designers who cultivated the space over the years.

Living plants

Not just a beautiful setting, The Huntington is also a centre of research with a deservedly hyped rare corpse flower collection, whose tall, short-lived stinky bloom was last witnessed in June 2022, as well as a weekly rotation of rare specimens from the holdings of over 10,000 orchid plants. Less well-known but still mind-blowing is their focus on cycad species, a living fossil that dates back hundreds of millions of years and propagates by cone.

Opposite: Balboa Park's Botanical Building is made of lath (thin strips of wood)

Right: The Huntington hosts touring exhibitions, such as Nasa's *Orbit Pavilion* in 2016

© BLACOGRAF / SHUTTERSTOCK

Beyond the flowers

Lovers of art and the humanities should save time for perusing the non-botanical collections, with such riches as a Gutenberg Bible and books by Marco Polo in the Huntington Library and works by Edward Hopper and Thomas Gainsborough in the art museum. But, for plant lovers the opportunity to traverse the world, whether to Oceania via the Australian Garden or closer to home via the California Garden is exhilarating. It's a cross-section of Earth packed into one small corner of SoCal.

Don't Miss

➡ **Strolling among koi-filled ponds and gingko trees in the Japanese Garden**

➡ **Savouring afternoon tea in the Rose Garden Tea Room**

➡ **Admiring golden barrel cacti planted from seed before 1915**

Find Your Joy

Getting there

LA's Gold Line Metro to Allen drops you a couple of miles from The Huntington; from there you can walk, bike or taxi.

Accessibility

All buildings and most garden areas at The Huntington are accessible to wheelchairs. Wheelchairs are also available to rent.

When to go

July and August can be hot. Visit in January or February for the camellias; March for flowering magnolia, peach, redbud and trumpet trees; and late November or early December for vibrant yellow ginkgos. The roses stay in bloom from summer to autumn.

Further information

• Admission charge. No reservations required weekdays; weekends require a prebooked timed ticket.
• Open year-round except for holidays; closed Tue.
• No dogs allowed, except service dogs.
• Dining available on site; no picknicking.
• https://huntington. org/

Other Southern Californian Gardens

Los Angeles County Arboretum & Botanic Garden

This sprawling botanic garden is also a wildlife sanctuary beloved by birders and the resident peafowl. It's notable for rambling roses and an incredible grove of over 250 Engelmann Oaks, the largest left in LA County. Plants from the Canary Islands and Madagascar showcase species from around the world.

Don't miss

Relaxing next to the splashing Meyberg Waterfall

Balboa Park Gardens

Located in sunny San Diego's most famous park, these free, themed gardens include a beautiful Japanese Garden, a Palm Canyon with 50 species, the Florida Canyon depicting the area's prehispanic landscape and the Alcazar Garden whose tiles, fountains and formal planting were inspired by its namesake in Seville.

Don't miss

Gasping at the huge, century-old Moreton Bay Fig

Gush over waterfalls and tropical botany

♡ Thundering cascades, exhilaration, rescued fauna

🕐 September

A s you meander along the path through cloud forest, ferns curl at your feet and bromeliads explode overhead. Stepping onto a platform for a closer view of a lofty waterfall, cool mist drifts down and clings to your face. Among the flower gardens, the sweet fragrance of pink gingers and frenetic buzz of hummingbirds carry on the breeze. Welcome to La Paz Waterfall Gardens, an oasis that evokes elation and awe, where wandering around feels like starring in your own Costa Rican fairy tale.

Growing pains

Hidden away on the slope of the Poás Volcano, these 70 enchanting acres (28 hectares) undulate from 3940ft to 4920ft

(1200-1500m) and once belonged to a rancher who kept cattle, horses and goats. The volcanic soil and cold climate weren't amenable to most tropical plants and frequent rain would wash away all but the most stubborn specimens, but when ambitious US entrepreneur Lee Banks purchased the property in the 1990s, he wanted a garden.

Banks and his employees brought in thousands of gingers, heliconias and other lowland plants, and followed the accepted guidance for maintaining these delicate beauties. Within a few months, nearly all of them had died. Disappointed, Banks removed them and followed his neighbours' lead, planting altitude-appropriate species like calla lilies, canna lilies, hydrangeas and mountain

COSTA RICA

Right: The 85ft (26m) Templo fall is the third tallest of the five waterfalls in the park

Below: A mossy, misty trail; spot hummingbirds such as the green-crowned brilliant

© XENIA_PHOTOGRAPHY / SHUTTERSTOCK

© BOIVIN NICOLAS / SHUTTERSTOCK

Q&A

What made you want to create this garden?
The idea was to bring together all the best flowers from Costa Rica's Pacific and Caribbean coasts so that people who don't have time to travel throughout the country could see everything. It didn't work! But we definitely created something unique.

Tell us something special about the garden.
Absolutely. There's a secret design to the layout, and that's to make hummingbirds cross the path of humans. If you identify the nectar plants, you'll see that they crisscross, and we also used plants that hummingbirds can perch on.

What's your top tip for enjoying the garden?
The Peace Lodge offers 18 rooms so stay overnight and have the whole place to yourself in the early mornings and late afternoons. That's when the garden is at its most peaceful.

Lee Banks, La Paz Waterfall Gardens Nature Park Owner

© ONDREJ PROSICKY / SHUTTERSTOCK

© ERIC MIDDELKOOP / SHUTTERSTOCK

Right: Is it a dream? The Kroya fall in Sambangan's Secret Garden

Left: As well as jaguars there's a ranarium, a serpentarium, an aviary and a monkey habitat

two pools, a trout pond and an animal rescue centre filled with Costa Rica's most charismatic creatures. Today, visitors admire blue morphos in a butterfly observatory, engage hummingbirds with feeders and watch jaguars devour fresh meat.

A trail cuts through the forest, flanked by micro-orchids and punctuated with platforms overlooking a series of five stunning waterfalls. They range from 65ft to 120ft (20-37m) tall and the path presents views of these aquatic splendours from every angle. In the presence of water this powerful, there's a feeling of unmitigated solace.

Although these gardens are already a major draw, Banks is continuously making them better. The newest addition is a cathedral-like spa beside the lake, with yoga, meditation and steam rooms. Each day it's filled with gingers and heliconias, because there's no such thing as too many tropical flowers.

Don't Miss

→ **Appreciating the colours and textures of rare bromeliads**

→ **Feeling waterfall mist on your hands and face**

→ **Spending the night and having the place mostly to yourself**

papyrus, all of which did well. He added flowering banana plants and dozens of species of rare, high-elevation bromeliads that neighbours gifted him. A year later came a surprise: several hardy buds from the tropical lowland plants surfaced beneath the other plants. Banks cloned those, scattered them around and watched them thrive.

More than just a garden

The plants were just the beginning. Over the years, Banks added a five-star hotel, Peace Lodge, three restaurants,

Find Your Joy

Getting there

The park is an hour's drive from Juan Santamaría International Airport. You can take an early morning bus from capital San

José's Terminal del Caribe that's bound for Puerto Viejo de Sarapiquí – make sure it passes through Vara Blanca, and ask the driver to stop at La Paz. Wait in the same spot for the return bus.

Accessibility

Much of the nature park is wheelchair accessible, with the exception of the waterfall trail. Staff

members can transport guests with disabilities around the property in golf carts.

When to go

Heliconias and flowering bananas are most vibrant in April; forest vines and bromeliads pop in September and October. From May to August, the waterfalls are in full flow; September sees them

turn white, dropping into blue-green pools.

Further information
• Admission charge.
• Open year-round.
• No dogs allowed.
• Dining on site.
• https://waterfall gardens.com

Other Waterfall Gardens

Sambangan's Secret Garden, Indonesia

At this North Bali garden the point is to get soaking wet. Your adventure begins with a guided walk through rice paddies and marigold fields and down a stone stairway into a dramatic canyon, where the first and largest of seven waterfalls, Aling-aling, pours from on high. Subsequent attractions include cliff jumps into a cerulean lagoon.

Don't miss
Whooshing down the natural waterslide

Shaw Park Garden & Waterfall, Jamaica

A majestic cascade tumbles down the rocks at the centre of Shaw Park, just outside the town of Ocho Rios. Surrounding it is a large, tiered garden with 600 flower species. Standouts include brilliant bougainvillea, regal palms, fragrant hibiscus and twisting ferns, and as the park is situated atop a hill, there are views of Ocho Rios and the coastline.

Don't miss
Picnicking beside the waterfall

Hike inside a blooming volcano crater

 Tropical plants, immersion, fragrance

 April

USA (HAWAII)

While eastern Oʻahu is best known for snorkelling and bodysurfing, it's walking the 2.3-mile (3.7km) loop trail inside Koko Crater that will appeal to plant lovers.

Here you'll find tropical colours, intense fragrances and bizarre shapes that invade and intrigue the senses, from yellow and pink plumeria to bat-pollinated African sausage trees and sprawling octopus cacti. The plant collections here take up 60 acres (24 hectares) of the volcanic crater, with the crater rim towering high all around.

Plumeria immersion

The relatively easy, family friendly track climbs gently into, then around, the crater, beginning with a trail through the spectacular plumeria grove. Plumeria (also known as frangipani) may not be native to Hawaii, first introduced from tropical America in 1860, but it is Hawaii that made this sweet-scented, delicate-looking flower its own by presenting plumeria *leis* (garlands of flowers) to visitors in the early days of the tourism industry.

When Hawaii's own William Moragne discovered how to cross-pollinate plumeria in 1953, he produced a proliferation of glorious new colours and scents that soon associated plumeria with the growing excitement of travel to tropical Hawaii.

Koko Crater's stunning collection is arranged by colour: from whites, yellows, and pinks to deep reds. Next up along the trail are the equally vibrant bougainvillea and hibiscus.

Right: To get the heart pumping, tag on a 'staircase' climb to the rim of Koko Crater

Below: Koko Crater is an extinct tuff cone; plumeria flowers are especially fragrant at night

© OKIMO / SHUTTERSTOCK

© JASON C-K. CHAN / SHUTTERSTOCK

Q&A

What is your favourite plant?
I love the blood-red plumeria. There aren't many blooms on the tree, yet each one is so fragrant.

Nice. Many people would call that a frangipani.
We say plumeria. It's called *pua melia* in Hawaiian. *Pua* is flower and *melia* comes from 'meria'.

Got it. How did frang...I meean plumeria become so popular?
During the 'Boat Days' of the 1930s, *lei* sellers would line the streets leading to the piers where the boatloads of tourists docked. The popular *lei* was plumeria, because it grew in everyone's backyards. It was easy to string into *lei*, and most plumeria are very hardy. They don't fade as quickly as some other flowers.

Leis are still worn?
I don't go on stage without them. Plumeria is also known as 'the hula dancer's flower'.

Kanoe Miller, Former professional hula dancer, teacher

© PHILLIP B. ESPINASSE / SHUTTERSTOCK

A gentle climb

The trail passes plants from the Pacific, into cacti from the Americas, where there is a focus on the ability of desert plants to adapt to their environment. The intriguing tubby barrel cactus, which expands or contracts depending on rainfall, has leaves that can become 'spines' to reduce water transpiration.

Just past the trail's high point are rare and endangered flora of the Hawaiian Islands. Hawaii has 1400 native plants, but because of its remoteness, these species developed in isolation, and nearly 90% are found nowhere else in the world.

Keep an eye out for the *koki'o*, a spectacular red member of the hibiscus family, known for its nectar. The leaves of the *koa* tree are shaped to conserve water, while canoes, paddles and bowls were crafted from its trunk. The *ma'o*, or Hawaiian Cotton, has lovely yellow flowers used to make dyes and medicine.

Opposite: The awesome backdrop of Ho'omaluhia Botanical Garden

Right: The sheltered basin of the volcano is an ideal place to cultivate rare dryland plants

© MARINA POUSHKINA / SHUTTERSTOCK

On the way home

The descent passes through sections of curious and unusual plants from Madagascar, such as the eye-catching baobab, with its orange-red flowers, and the spectacular spiny trunked *pachypodiums*. Don't miss the peculiar fruit of the sausage tree in the Africa grouping.

As you complete the trail and head out of the crater be sure to look behind you at the dormant volcano you've just been inside, and marvel at what has felt like an exploratory voyage to another world.

Don't Miss

→ Searching out the 'Lei Rainbow', a plumeria with a strong sweet scent

→ Spotting hikers high on the crater rim

→ Admiring yellow *Ma'o hau hele*, the state flower of Hawaii

Find Your Joy

Getting there

There's a car park at the entrance, or take Bus 23 from the Ala Moana Center via Hawaii Kai to 'Kealahou St, opposite Kalohelani Pl' bus stop; it's a 10-minute walk from there.

Accessibility

The full path, within the volcanic crater, is rocky, uneven and sloping, not suitable for wheelchairs. The Plumeria Grove is close to the car park and reasonably accessible.

When to go

While the gardens are lovely year-round; plumerias bloom April to September, bougainvillea from September to April.

Further information

• Free admission.
• Open daily, year-round, except Christmas Day & New Year's Day.
• No dogs allowed.
• No cafe or restaurant on site. Bring your own water, as no drinking water available; portable toilet only.
• www.honolulu.gov/parks/hbg

Other Hawaiian Botanical Gardens

Ho`omaluhia Botanical Garden

Sitting right below the ridged *pali* (cliffs) of the Ko`olau mountain range, on the Windward Coast of O`ahu, these huge sprawling gardens feature plantings from tropical regions around the world. *Ho`omaluhia* means 'to make a place of peace and tranquillity' in Hawaiian, and this location makes for a memorable experience.

Don't miss
The views looking back towards the sheer cliffs over Loko Waimaluhia reservoir

Wahiawā Botanical Garden

In the central O`ahu town of Wahiawā, this attractive 27-acre (11-hectare) garden is one of the five beautifully maintained Honolulu County botanical gardens. Wahiawā is on a high plateau between the Wai'anae and Ko`olau mountain ranges, and the gardens are home to tropical flora that thrives in a cooler upland environment.

Don't miss
The views from the pedestrian bridge over the ravine

Asia

Fall into one man's labyrinthine imagination

♡ Outsider art, upcycled sculptures, inspiration

🕐 October to November

INDIA

Nek Chand's Rock Garden in Chandigarh is like nowhere else on Earth. Imagine prising open an artist's head and climbing into their imagination – that's the experience of diving into this surreal collection of sculptures, fantasy pavilions and maze-like pathways.

Though there's hardly a flower bed in sight, a hoarder's trove of recycled rubbish has been transformed into a fascinating facsimile of real life. It's the kind of garden an astronaut marooned on the moon would build as a reminder of home – an apt analogy perhaps, as this was all the work of just one person.

A singular vision
It takes a unique mind – and a certain confidence – to build a garden from rubbish, but municipal worker Nek Chand Saini was never one for doing things by the rules. While working as a road inspector for Chandigarh's Public Works Department, he constructed his astonishing rock garden in secret, using junk and leftover building materials from the construction of architect Le Corbusier's concept city.

Even more amazingly, this unusual garden lay undiscovered for a generation, hidden away in a gorge on the outskirts of the city. Nek Chand weaved his fantasy in private, using concrete, wiring, broken ceramics, bathroom components, and anything else he could lay his hands on. Over thousands of hours, herds of mosaic horses, crowds of concrete monkeys

Right: Nek Chand's figures are formed from sculpted concrete adorned with scrap material

Below: Chand also designed a series of lush waterfalls, pathways and pavilions

Q&A

What feeling do you get from the Rock Garden?
It is a very spiritual place – to realise this is the work of one man is very moving, particularly considering the endless struggles Nek Chand had with the Chandigarh Administration to keep the garden safe from development.

He certainly redefines 'secret hobby'. Why does the garden feel like a village?
Chandigarh is a city of refugees, and the Rock Garden reflects the village that Nek Chand had to flee in Pakistan. Nek Chand was also inspired by childhood stories of kings and queens and he wanted to make his own kingdom.

He rules. Where did he find his materials?
Nek Chand believed in turning waste into beauty. Not only did he use the remains of the 26 villages demolished to make way for the new city of Chandigarh, he also developed a network of collection points for anything from human hair to old bicycles and electrical fittings.

John Maizos, Nek Chand Foundation

© SAIKO3P / SHUTTERSTOCK

and broken crockery villagers emerged into the landscape, unseen by the residents of India's first planned modern city.

Saved by serendipity

That the garden still exists today is a consequence of public goodwill. When Nek Chand's unauthorised endeavour was discovered in 1975, the city authorities considered demolishing the entire site, but local people rallied round.

Instead of destroying it, the city's Chief Commissioner designated it a public space, appointing the former road inspector to the role of 'Sub-Divisional Engineer, Rock Garden'.

Down the rabbit hole

Exploring the garden today is an *Alice in Wonderland*-like journey along meandering pathways, passing anthropomorphic pebble people, dangling rope swings, tinkling waterfalls and banks covered by legions of mosaic villagers and a vast menagerie of

Opposite: *The Monolith*, one of many mind-bending artworks at Frognerparken

Right: Nek Chand's sculptures now appear in museums around the world

sculpted animals, from cement elephants to broken-glass birdlife.

At times, the experience is beautiful; at other times, it's almost uncanny being under the gaze of so many unblinking ceramic eyes. Working out what each sculpture is made of – an electrical transformer, a toilet cistern, a broken teacup? – is part of the experience. In the process, you'll re-examine your preconceptions about beauty, art, rubbish, the definition of a garden, and the value of a human perspective when nature is subverted by architecture.

Don't Miss

➡ **Swinging on rope swings in the garden's cement arches**

➡ **Wandering through herds of handcrafted livestock**

➡ **Admiring sparkling costumes of glass bangle dancers**

Find Your Joy

Getting there

The Rock Garden is in Sector 1, on the northeast edge of Chandigarh. Come by taxi or autorickshaw, or walk here through the city's orderly grid of streets.

Accessibility

This maze of concrete and cobble pathways might not seem ideal for visitors with mobility issues, but the municipal government is slowly adding ramps, railings, Braille signs, accessible toilets and other amenities for visitors with disabilities.

When to go

There's no off-season for a garden made from recycled rubbish, but the climate can have a major effect. The pre-monsoon months of April and May are oven-hot, and once the monsoon breaks, expect heavy rain and humidity from June to September. October and November are good times to visit.

Further information

• Admission charge.
• Open daily, year-round, with longer hours from April to September.
• No dogs allowed.
• No cafe, but vendors sell snacks and drinks.
• https://chandigarhtourism.gov.in/pages/page/rock-garden

Other Singular Sculpture Gardens

Tarot Garden, Italy

A great sculpture garden needs a vision, and that's the case at the Tarot Garden in Pescia Fiorentina in Tuscany. French-American artist Niki de Saint Phalle moulded these vivid sculptural depictions of the 22 major arcana of the divinatory tarot in 1979, drawing inspiration from Gaudí's Parc Güell in Barcelona.

Don't miss

The hallucinatory figure of the *Empress* – de Saint Phalle lived inside it for seven years while constructing her fantasy garden

Vigeland Installation, Norway

Over nearly 40 years, Norwegian sculptor Gustav Vigeland filled a corner of Frognerparken in Oslo with more than 200 sculptures, centred on *The Monolith*, a totem-pole-like pillar writhing with human figures. It's a remarkable monument to one man's creative vision.

Don't miss

The sculpture of a naked man being attacked by angry babies

© ESPEN GRØNLI / COURTESY OF FROGNERPARKEN

Follow in the footsteps of scholars

CHINA

  Rockeries, relaxation, poetic views

April to June

Willow branches waft across craggy rockeries. Water trickles over smooth rocks. A pebble path leads to a row of bonsai trees. And a lattice window presents a perfectly framed view of a distant pagoda. This is the Humble Administrator's Garden, grandest of all classical Chinese gardens, designed as a place of tranquillity, where scholars and poets could think, write and drink tea.

Perfect irregularity

Unlike in Imperial Chinese architecture, nothing inside the Humble Administrator's Garden is symmetrical – rather, design elements are purposely skewed. There's an uncertainty in the scale too, which creates a playful tension that keeps your interest

as you wander. In many places, one thing is designed to be viewed through something else: powder-blue sky through holes in rocks; leaves reflected on water; a whimsical bridge seen through a window. In classical Chinese garden design, this is known as the 'borrowed view from afar'.

Of scholars past

Though a garden of some kind has been here since the Shaoxing period (1131-1162), its current form dates to the early 1500s when the 'humble administrator' himself, imperial envoy Wang Xiancheng, converted the pre-existing garden into his retirement villa. The 12.8-acre (5.2-hectare) garden is cluttered with zigzagging bridges, bamboo groves, lotus ponds, stone mosaic pathways and at least 10 airy

Q&A

What was a scholar's garden?
They were private retreats where retired scholar-officials spent their golden years writing, painting and conversing with other literati.

How are gardens like Lan Su and the Humble Administrator's Garden similar?
Lan Su borrows key elements from the Humble Administrator's Garden. Both adhere to Song and Ming-dynasty aesthetics and landscape architecture, with a central pond traversed by stone bridges, rockeries that serve as miniature mountain ranges, and intimate side gardens and passageways.

What do you love most about Chinese gardens?
The way the natural and built environments are intertwined – you're never completely indoors or outdoors.

Best tip for enjoying a classical Chinese garden?
Looking at classical Chinese landscape paintings, such as those of Wen Zhengming, before your visit will enhance your experience in the garden.

Gabriel Forest Weiss, Architectural Conservator, Lan Su Chinese Garden

© ZHAROV PAVEL / LONELY PLANET

Right: The tranquil perfection of Lan Su Chinese Garden

Left: Moon gates frame scenes in a classical Chinese garden and invite you to step into them

Don't Miss

→ Enjoying the rich fragrance of blooming lotus wafting through pavilions

→ Walking across Small Flying Rainbow Bridge

→ Admiring the circular view through the round Moon Gate

pavilions whose poetic names ('Listening to the Sound of Rain'; 'Celestial Spring') evoke the feelings and sensations designed to be experienced within them. Entering the Humble Administrator's Garden feels like stepping into a three-dimensional scroll painting, and, indeed, the garden was beloved by painter, calligrapher and writer Wen Zhengming, who immortalised it in words and paintings in the 16th century.

Scholars who built such gardens incorporated water, stone, plants and architecture to create an idealised version of nature, a beautifully configured microcosm of the fundamental aspects of the natural world. Wherever you stand, you take in a particular scene, like a page in a shifting folio of paintings. Every few steps, a new composition emerges, framed by the architecture, foliage or stonework.

Sunlight and seasons

Classical Chinese gardens are designed to bloom in every season, whether the delicate pond lotus in summer or the yellow flowers of Chinese paperbush in winter. Even the shifting of sunlight throughout the day can dramatically alter the garden's appearance, with lengthening shadows creating new shapes. During a rainstorm, the drip tiles that line the eaves of the pavilion roofs create shimmering, singing curtains of water, like long strings of pearls. The garden is ever-changing – by the hour, day and season.

Find Your Joy

Getting there

High-speed trains run between Shanghai and Suzhou in 25 minutes. The Suzhou Metro connects to Beisita station (Line 4), a 20-minute walk from the Humble Administrator's Garden. A taxi or ride-share from the station takes around 30 minutes outside of rush hour.

Accessibility

The garden is wheelchair-friendly, with a dedicated sightseeing route offering access to most of the garden along a flat, paved path. There's also an accessible toilet in the visitor centre.

When to go

Visit in June for the Rhododendron Festival; from July to September for the Lotus Festival. Low season from November to February is best for a more serene experience with fewer crowds.

Further information

• Admission charge; passport required.
• Open year-round.
• No dogs allowed.
• Teahouses on site.
• Name in Chinese: 拙政园 (Zhuōzhèng Yuán).

Other Chinese Gardens

Lan Su Chinese Garden, USA

Lan Su in Portland, Oregon, is one of the finest examples of a classical, Suzhou-style garden outside of China. Designed by experts from Suzhou, it's based on the Humble Administrator's Garden, with native Chinese plants such as magnolia, peony and osmanthus infusing colour throughout the year.

Don't miss

Taking a tour to discover the garden's symbolic details and rich history

Lan Yuan, New Zealand

New Zealand's only authentic Chinese garden and the first of its kind in the Southern Hemisphere, Lan Yuan opened in Dunedin in 1998. Designed to commemorate the Chinese people who came here during the 1860s gold rush, it was constructed in Shanghai and shipped to its new home.

Don't miss

Spotting traditional decorations including tiles, bricks, lattice-work and granite paving stones

Meditate in a Korean *bunjae* garden

♡ Fascination, design, culture

🕐 April and May

SOUTH KOREA

As you enter the Spirited Garden, it's as if you've passed through a portal into a fantasy botanical world. You'll feel delight and wonder as you stand on a bridge gazing down into a pond teeming with golden carp. Basalt stone pathways lead you through a landscape of pines, palms, lawns, meditative areas and waterfalls. And all around, displayed in pots, are artfully contorted miniature trees and shrubs: *bunjae*, the Korean style of bonsai.

Spirited Garden on Jeju-do, South Korea's largest island, is famous for its collection of some 2000-plus *bunjae*. Contemplation of these exquisite natural sculptures, some of which are hundreds of years old, is a practice which can bring a deep sense of peace. Stand back to admire the overall shape of the *bunjae*. Stoop low to appreciate the detail of its form. The sturdiness of the roots and trunks, the asymmetry of the branches, the unique shape of leaves, the blossoms and fruit – each *bunjae* is a work of art.

A life-long passion

The garden is a perfect example of Korean pioneering spirit. In 1968, Sung Bum-young, a 29-year-old tailor from Seoul, bought an unpromising piece of land, littered with thistles and volcanic rocks, on Jeju. From this forbidding landscape, he first hacked out a citrus farm while simultaneously nurturing a dream to create a garden showcasing *bunjae*. You need patience to craft these living

Right: The volcanic soil and tropical climate of Jeju-do make it ideal for growing tangerines

Below: *Bunjae* trees great and small; any tree species can be formed into a *bunjae*

© STEVE JANGS / SHUTTERSTOCK

© SPIRITED GARDEN

Q&A

What's special about *bunjae*?
My father has spent over 50 years creating and tending this garden. He says *bunjae* can be thought of as an act of seeking the truth of life, leading the human soul closer to its origin, Mother Nature.

How are *bunjae* different from Japanese bonsai?
The art of bonsai started in China about 3000 years ago, passed through Korea, and then went to Japan. Bonsai is on a large scale in China, while in Japan it is delicate. Korean *bunjae* find a middle ground.

What's written on the plaques by each *bunjae*?
They are about what my father has learned from the plants that he has taken care of over the past half century. Each of them has a different story, and they speak quietly to the heart.

Sung Ju-yeop, General Manager and son of the creator of Spirited Garden

sculptures, which can take many decades to come into their prime, and as well as growing his own *bunjae*, Sung scoured Korea for others to add to his collection. Since opening in 1992 the garden's reputation has grown – as has the garden itself, with a recently added section focused on a 500-year-old juniper tree.

Opposite: Water spills down a lava rock wall in Hallim Park

Right: *Dolharubang* sculptures protect against demons and are a symbol of Jeju-do

© JONG-WON HEO / GETTY IMAGES

Admire the rock art

Amping up Spirited Garden's surreal atmosphere is its rock art. In a nod to local island culture, there are several *dolharubang* (grandfather rocks). These guardians of the landscape have the traditional broad noses and bug eyes associated with this type of sculpture, along with phallus-like helmets, which make it easy to see why they're considered fertility symbols.

Other structures made from Jeju's signature black basalt include a seven-storey ziggurat, a gateway with a stunning bronze gate, and the fortress-like stone perimeter walls. These are there for a purpose – to protect the tender *bunjae* and other plants from the typhoons and winds that gust off the East China Sea.

A taste of citrus

The citrus trees, including mandarins, tangerines and kumquats that Sung originally cultivated on this land, still have a place in his garden. In April, breathe in the piquant aromas of the blossoms; throughout the year, sip a glass of sweet tangerine tea in the cafe.

Don't Miss

→ Feeding the carp in the ornamental ponds

→ Taking a photo beside the world's biggest *dolharubang* (grandfather rock)

→ Climbing up to the observatory for a panoramic view of the garden

Find Your Joy

Getting there
Spirited Garden is 22 miles (35km) southwest of Jeju International Airport. If driving it will take about 50 minutes; by bus 2 hours.

Accessibility
There are a few gentle slopes and narrow paths in the garden, but otherwise it is fairly easy to get around for those with mobility issues, including wheelchair users.

When to go
There's year-round interest in the garden. Visit in April for the cherry blossom; in May, wisteria blooms are at their finest. The fruit of the quince trees ripens from October and the tangerines from November.

Further information
• Admission charge.
• Open year-around.
• No dogs over 11lbs (5kg) allowed.
• Korean restaurant and a cafe are on site.
• www.spiritedgarden.com

Other Gardens on Jeju

Hallim Park

This park west of Jeju city has nine different themed areas including a subtropical botanical garden and a road edged with skyscraping palms. The flower collection runs from daffodils and narcissi in January to chrysanthemums in November and camellias in December.

Don't miss

The stone and *bunjae* garden where a collection of rare rocks are surrounded by tiny pine, quince and ancient maple trees

Halla Arboretum

This 37-acre (15-hectare) botanical garden is one of the best spots on the island for forest bathing. Follow a wooden decking trail between strands of bamboo and be enchanted by the fuzzy green splendour of the moss garden. There's a small glasshouse devoted to orchids, as well as aquatic plants and wildflowers.

Don't miss

The greenhouse with vivid emerald ferns contrasting against black basalt rocks

Wander through a wafting bamboo forest

CHINA

❤ Peace, fresh air, mountain views

🕐 April and May

*Clinging to verdant
mountains without ceasing,
The bamboo stays rooted
in rock crevices.
Through many blows,
it stands strong,
Defying winds from
every direction.*
Zhen Xie, *Bamboo in the Rocks*.
Translated by Megan Eaves.

Tall and thin, their sectioned culms rise like green lamp posts, hundreds in every direction. In the canopy above, leaves sway in the breeze, imitating the sound of a phantom stream. You look up and the shoots seem to mesh with the sky, dappling the forest floor with coins of sunlight. A stone path leads up steps, deeper into the emerald grove. This is Anji Bamboo Sea in the mountains of eastern Zhejiang province, one of the largest such forests in China.

Magical, regenerative shoots
One of the 'four noble plants' (along with chrysanthemum, orchid and plum), bamboo is native to the country and symbolises vitality and integrity. This woody grass has been grown in China for over 7000 years and has over 1400 species, including giant moso bamboo, native to Anji. Bamboo is the fastest-growing plant on Earth. It absorbs 30% more carbon dioxide and releases 30% more oxygen than leafy trees, and can be harvested every three to five years. Its roots stop soil erosion and its timber is almost as strong as steel. Bamboo shoots provide nutritious and tasty food

Right: A trail leads into the rustling green of the Bamboo Sea

Below: The Bamboo Sea contains 27 mountains; over 70% of Anji County is made up of forest

© VIEWSTOCK / GETTY IMAGES

© DANDESIGN86 / SHUTTERSTOCK

Q&A

How did you get interested in bamboo?
I've always believed it's one of the best examples of how natural resources help sustainable development. It's good for the environment (soil conservation, biodiversity); for people (jobs, food, shelter); and for the economy (lots of products).

What were your impressions of Anji Bamboo Sea?
The bamboo culms in Anji are tall and flexible and the wind makes a mesmerising sound through the leaves.

Any cool facts about bamboo?
A Chinese species of bamboo is the fastest-growing plant in the world – around 3ft (1m) per day.

Dr Hans Friederich, Ambassador of the World Bamboo Organisation

© MEGAN EAVES

© DAN HANSCOM / SHUTTERSTOCK

Right: Savour the meditative soundscape of Sagano Bamboo Forest

Left: Anji forest is home to around 40 species of bamboo

Don't Miss

→ Climbing the lookout tower for expansive mountain views

→ Finding the filming location for *Crouching Tiger, Hidden Dragon*

→ Sampling buttery, tender, stir-fried bamboo shoots

and it can be made into clothing. Every year, 12 million canes of this extraordinary plant are extracted from Anji's forests, providing the area's main economy.

Forest of green

Bamboo has carpeted the mountains of Anji County for millennia – archaeological remains show Anji's natural bamboo forests represented with ideograms more than 5000 years ago. In the 1990s, a 230-sq-mile (600-sq-km) section was designated as the Anji Bamboo Sea, with walkways allowing

easy access. Not a traditionally landscaped garden, this place is a wild ecological preservation area full of natural, mountain bamboo groves. The tourist infrastructure includes a zip line and glass bridge, but it's easy to leave those behind, straying down paths to places hidden on the mountainsides, where human voices are replaced by birdsong and the rustling of bamboo leaves, leaving you invigorated from all the extra oxygen produced by the bamboo.

Big screen bamboo cameo

If you can't make it to Anji, you can experience the Bamboo Sea by watching Ang Lee's *Crouching Tiger, Hidden Dragon*. The two main characters, Jen and Mu Bai, float across the tops of the forest canopy in a martial arts dance, the bamboo providing a hypnotising backdrop. Arriving at Anji Bamboo Sea today, you're greeted by a huge rock carved with the film's Chinese name: 卧虎藏龙.

Find Your Joy

Getting there

Buses (every 20 minutes; taking 40 minutes) run from the bus station in Dipu, Anji County's main town. Anji can be

reached by high-speed railway from Huzhou, which has train and plane connections to other parts of China.

Accessibility

The garden is in a mountain area and is generally not accessible for wheelchairs. Stone and dirt paths and steps lead through the forest, often up steep inclines.

When to go

Bamboo is evergreen, so the Anji Bamboo Sea can be visited year-round. The best season is from March to May, when new growth is sprouting and before summer's crowds descend. This is also the best time to taste fresh, stir-fried bamboo shoots, a local delicacy.

Further information

• Admission charge.
• Open year-round.
• Dogs welcome on a lead.
• Teahouse on site.
• Name in Chinese: 安吉大竹海 (Ānjí Dàzhúhǎi)

Other Bamboo Gardens

Bambouseraie en Cévennes, France

Horticulturalist Eugène Mazel planted this grove in 1856, bringing bamboo to the south of France from East Asia and North America. Later purchased and further developed by Gaston Nègre and his son, today the garden includes over 1000 species of bamboo, a Zen garden, a hedge maze, the original greenhouses that Mazel built, a Laotian-style village and a shop with bamboo items.

Don't miss

Wandering through the rockeries and pavilions in the Valley of the Dragon Japanese garden

Sagano Bamboo Forest, Japan

On the northwest outskirts of Kyoto stands Sagano, one of the most photographed bamboo forests in the world. Its peaceful pathways twist through miles of natural, moso bamboo groves, which make such a wonderful rustling noise that the Japanese Ministry of the Environment designated it as one of the '100 Soundscapes of Japan'.

Don't miss

Smelling the incense at 14th-century Tenryu-ji Temple, just outside the forest gates

Savour the green at Koke-dera's moss garden

JAPAN

♡ Serenity, history, Zen design

🕐 June to mid-July

In western Kyōto, the Zen temple Saihō-ji is commonly known as Koke-dera, meaning 'moss temple', for its legendary expanses of the green and spongy ground plant. This is a place for those who love all shades of green, but in true Zen style, you're going to have to go through a few hardships to get to the lush paradise.

Serendipitous moss

According to temple legend, Saihō-ji was originally constructed in 731, during the Nara Period, but over the years, fell into disrepair. It was then restored in 1339 as a Zen temple, landscaped by renowned poet and garden designer Musō Soseki, but without moss in the concept. It is believed to have had a beautiful pavilion overlooking the pond and a graceful arched bridge. It was planted with cherry trees and weeping willows, along with pine trees. Falling into disrepair again and with the monastery having insufficient funds for its upkeep, the story goes that the moss we see today took over of its own accord.

Peaceful pilgrimage

The moss garden was first opened to the public in 1928, and until 1977 was open to everyone on a walk-up basis, as with other temples in Kyōto. It became so popular however, that Saihō-ji became an early example of sustainable tourism, by deciding to limit

Right: Moss loves damp and shady conditions and can absorb up to 20 times its weight in liquid

Below: Visitors are restricted to protect the delicate site; a garden well

© JULIAN52000 / SHUTTERSTOCK

© FANG CHUNKAI / SHUTTERSTOCK

Q&A

What makes Koke-dera so special?
The moss has not been deliberately planted. Over the centuries, the temple was ravaged by war and flooding. Nature, in the form of the moss, eventually took over. The 120 species of moss grow here naturally. Many species have a symbiotic relationship with each other. It is a happy place for moss. Hopefully climate change is not going to ruin this.

Let's hope. Unhappy moss is not what we want. What are your favourite aspects of the garden?
Each species of moss lends its own unique shade of green and texture. This creates a subtle play of light and shade, together with any sunlight filtering down between the branches of the trees. Both the moss and the rocks look their most lustrous in the rain. Rain makes Japanese gardens very atmospheric. Don't let drizzle put you off visiting Saihō-ji.

Yoko Kawaguchi, Author of 'Japanese Zen Gardens'

© IRINA SMOLINA / SHUTTERSTOCK

numbers, in order to protect the moss garden and the integrity of the temple as a functioning Zen place of religious practice, with a peaceful atmosphere conducive to prayer and meditation.

An extremely convoluted reservation system was put in place, which requires plenty of forward planning, a high visiting fee (when compared with other temples in Kyōto) and most interesting of all, a requirement for all visitors to write out the Heart Sutra, using a brush and ink (visitors can trace over the Chinese characters on the printed page they are given) before entering the garden.

Opposite:
The temple at Ginkaku-ji was intended to be covered in silver

Right: The landscape and beauty of the moss garden have been likened to a Studio Ghibli film

© FANG CHUNKAI / SHUTTERSTOCK

A garden of green

Once visitors reach the promised land of the moss garden, they realise that it was all worth the effort. In the eastern temple grounds, the garden is arranged as a gorgeous circular promenade centered on Golden Pond, which is shaped like the Chinese character for 'heart' or 'mind' (*kokoro*). The moss is at its greenest during *tsuyu* (the rainy season, June to mid-July) and in early summer, when humidity in Kyōto is at its highest. Humidity levels over these seasons are also affected by the nearby Katsura River, and the air can feel both heavy and intense.

Turn up in autumn (October and November) though, and there's a remarkable contrast of colour, with the striking reds and oranges of the turning leaves contrasting the velvety carpet of greens below.

Don't Miss

→ **Admiring the moss-covered bridges**

→ **Photographing the green maples that turn red in autumn**

→ **Marvelling at the 104 screen paintings in the temple's main hall**

Find Your Joy

Getting there
Take Bus 73 from Kyōto station for an hour to 'Kokedera / Suzumushi-dera' bus stop; it's a 3-minute walk from there.

Accessibility
The garden is not wheelchair accessible, and is difficult for those with mobility issues. Paths are made of stone, are uneven and can be slippery.

When to go
During *Tsuyu*, the rainy season (June to mid-July), the moss is at its lustrous best; rain and humidity is good for moss. Come in October for autumn colours.

Further information
• Admission charge. Requires pre-booking two weeks before visit.
• The temple is open year-round, but the garden is closed mid-January to February.
• No dogs allowed.
• No cafe on site.

• www.saihoji-kokedera.com

Other Kyōto Temple Gardens

Ryōan-ji

The rock garden at the Zen temple Ryōan-ji (Temple of the Dragon at Peace) is so well known it has become synonymous with Japanese rock gardens worldwide. The simple layout of 15 stones atop white sand has been a riddle since its conception around 1500. Like a Zen puzzle, the meaning is left up to the viewer's imagination and interpretation.

Don't miss

Ryōan-ji's teahouse and tea garden

Ginkaku-ji

At the foot of Kyōto's eastern hills, the Zen temple Ginkaku-ji (Temple of the Silver Pavilion), which isn't actually silver, is known for its black pines and the Sea of Silvery Sand. This is a meticulously raked sand garden, in an art form known as *samon*. In moonlight its ridges appear as ripples in water.

Don't miss

The Mt Fuji look-alike, made of sand, that is carefully reconstructed each month

Behold a Mughal vision of heaven on Earth

♡ Water features, symmetry, awe

🕐 October to November

INDIA

The name Nishat Bagh means 'garden of joy' and that's a good indication of the thinking behind this gorgeous Mughal garden, created in 1633 by Asif Khan, the brother-in-law of Mughal emperor Jahangir. Floating between its colourful planted beds, gushing fountains and pool-filled terraces feels like slipping inside a Mughal miniature painting. Come in autumn, when the towering chinar trees burn bonfire-red, and joy is just one of the many emotions you'll experience.

Paradise on earth
Like many Mughal gardens, Nishat Bagh was conceived as a representation of the *char bagh* – the four gardens of paradise recorded in the Quran. However, the traditional Persian model of heaven had to be tweaked to fit this mountainous landscape. Instead of a square garden, Nishat Bagh cuts a slender transect through the Himalayan landscape, beckoning the eye downwards towards the misty waters of Dal Lake.

It's easy to picture the silk-clad men and women of the Mughal court retreating to its terraces to admire views towards the flooded Oont Kadal bridge and the distant fortress that stands guard over Srinagar, sipping on sherbet and feasting on sweet morsels amid the dahlias and roses.

The height of Islamic design
Despite the modified design, Nishat Bagh is a feast of Islamic details. Children splash about in its spring-fed central

Right: Two octagonal towers in the retaining walls of Nishat Bagh provide views of the lower terraces

Below: The beatific cascade of water and terraces; fiery chinar trees in autumn

© STASTNY_PAVEL / SHUTTERSTOCK

© PAKENEE KITTIPINYOWAT / SHUTTERSTOCK

My Garden Joy

Dropping down to Srinagar en route from Ladakh as the chill of autumn started to creep into the evenings, my first taste of Nishat Bagh was a revelation. I arrived with preconceptions of Kashmir as a place of violence, and found a place of profound peace and serenity, and of beauty. At Nishat Bagh, the last flowers of summer still lingered but the leaves of the towering chinar trees burned like a wildfire, carrying the promise of approaching winter. As I wandered the terraces, a young Kashmiri teacher fell in step and talked me through the history of the gardens like it was a family history, observing that the Mughal Empire produced as many poets as warriors. I left with a sense of inner peace that lingered throughout my time in Kashmir.

Joe Bindloss

© KADIA / SHUTTERSTOCK

© GENIUS STUDIO / SHUTTERSTOCK

Right: Each of the three terraces at Shalimar Bagh had a role

Left: Water flows from the 18ft (5.5m) facade of the 12th terrace, backed by mountains

Don't Miss

→ Enjoying views across the silvery waters of Dal Lake

→ Admiring the autumn colours of the chinar trees

→ Absorbing serene sunsets over the Kashmir Valley

watercourse, which slips over a series of *chadars* – washboard-like ripples designed to create the effect of a shawl made from swishing white water. On the highest terrace, Islamic arches mark the *zenana*, the private compound reserved for the family of Asif Khan.

The garden's 12 tumbling terraces stand in for the 12 months of the Muslim lunar calendar. Viewed from the top, a floral stairway drops to the mirror-flat surface of Dal Lake. Seen from the lake, the gardens climb through avenues of tall chinar

trees to a rugged mountain wall that winter caps with snow. Uplifting only just describes it.

A jealous treasure?
Nishat Bagh was built for a noble, rather than an emperor, so it lacks some of the lavish embellishments of Jahangir's private garden at nearby Shalimar Bagh, but it amply compensates with its lake-framed location. This is the sublime vision of Kashmir that greeted hippies who turned on, tuned in and dropped out in the 1960s, before downtown Srinagar became a gauntlet of houseboat agents.

Jahangir was reputedly so jealous of Nishat Bagh that he asked for the garden as a gift – and, when his request was refused, cut off the water supply. To see the garden as the Mughals did, take a ride on a canopy-covered *shikara* boat over the lilting waters of Dal Lake and view the garden from afar as autumn sets the chinar trees aflame.

Find Your Joy

Getting there
Nishat Bagh runs down to the shore of Dal Lake, 8 miles (13km) northeast of Srinagar. You can get here easily by taxi or local bus

and *shikara* boats wait for passengers at the jetty by the entrance to the gardens.

Accessibility
With its many steps, Nishat Bagh is not easily accessible for visitors with mobility issues and wheelchairs. Travel agencies in Srinagar should be able to arrange a guide who can assist

less able visitors up the terraces.

When to go
From September to November, the towering chinar trees turn vivid shades of red, yellow and amber, but flowers are most lush in spring. Avoid the rain-drenched monsoon months from June to September.

Further information
• Admission charge.
• Open daily except Friday, year-round.
• No dogs allowed.
• No cafe, but vendors sell snacks and drinks.
• https://srinagar.nic.in/tourist-place/nishat-garden

Other Mughal Gardens In India

Sunder Nursery

Featuring 4500 trees and 54 varieties of flowering plants, the 16th-century Sunder Nursery was almost lost to history under Delhi's urban sprawl, before a painstaking restoration project backed by the Aga Khan. Today the Mughal tombs gleam, surrounded by lush beds and water features, arranged in the Persian *char bagh* design.

Don't miss

Tracing the garden's watercourse along the route of the original Grand Trunk Rd

Shalimar Bagh

Srinagar's other great garden, Shalimar Bagh was built by the emperor Jahangir as a gift for his wife Nur Jahan in 1619. Its original name – Farah Baksh, meaning 'the delightful' – is an apt description. The elegant belvederes that once provided solace to a Mughal emperor are like dainty jewel boxes, set amid limpid pools.

Don't miss

The *chini khanas* – niches set behind waterfalls that once glowed with the flickering light of butter lamps

Be calmed by a lush, hi-tech indoor garden

♡ Topiary, waterfall, tranquillity

🕐 Year-round

SINGAPORE

When it comes to creating a focal feature for a garden, it's difficult to beat the wow factor of the Rain Vortex at the heart of Jewel Changi Airport. Your eyes will pop at the world's tallest indoor waterfall, a thundering monsoon plummeting 130ft (40m) through the air from a giant oculus in the funnel-shaped glass roof. Surrounding the waterfall is the Forest Valley where over 900 tall trees and palms and 60,000 shrubs sprout out of and cascade over four floors of this futuristic shopping mall attached to Singapore's Changi Airport. Arriving fresh from a long-distance flight, it can feel as if you've strolled into a scene from *Avatar*.

A full sensory experience

Feel any jet lag or worries fade away as you wander along either of the two cobblestoned trails through the multi-level Forest Valley. Daylight from the glazed ceiling filters through the tree branches to create dappled shade, and the roar of the Rain Vortex is supplemented by softer sound effects of raindrops and a flowing river.

As night falls, a hi-tech, light installation brightens things up. Rainbow-hued lights illuminate the foliage, increasing and decreasing in intensity as if the garden is breathing. Motion detectors adjust the colour tones subtly and softly as people move by, adding to the sense of serenity. A calming background soundtrack evokes

Right: The vibrant Petal Garden, displaying flowers from all over the world

Below: The Rain Vortex falls over seven storeys; flower sculptures dot the Topiary Walk

Q&A

What's your favourite bloom in the garden?
Tropical orchids are free-flowering year-round and they come in all sorts of vibrant colours, shape and sizes. I especially enjoy Oncidium 'Golden Shower' as it's a popular hybrid and has sentimental value for me. The flower spikes resemble yellow fireworks and look celebratory.

How are the topiary sculptures made?
Typically from fibreglass and covered with plant materials or part-artificial flowers. Some of them have recesses that allow us to place cacti or flowers.

I hear you also have a smoke bubble tree?
Yes, for the December holidays we install a 13ft (4m) smoke bubble tree in the Petal Garden. It's awesome to watch the bubbles fall from the tree and pop with a smoking effect.

Erinna Pak, Manager User Experience (Landscape)

the rhythmic lapping of ocean waves, and in the air is a gentle aroma that combines floral notes of rose and lotus – this is sponsor Shiseido's Ultimune scent, also designed to relieve stress.

Fun in the Canopy Park

The gardens at this climate-controlled mall are not solely about lowering your blood pressure and creating a sense of calm though. There are also sections to boost your energy and provide a bit of a thrill. For a bird's-eye view of the garden, walk across the Canopy Bridge. Suspended 75ft (23m) above the ground, the bridge's central glass-floor section is only for those with a head for heights, while the fog emitted at both ends of the bridge makes it feel like you're walking among the clouds.

In the Canopy Park on the mall's top floor are an array of themed garden attractions, some of which have separate

Opposite: The Supertrees in Gardens by the Bay provide a nightly light show

Right: Climb the watch tower in the centre of the Hedge Maze to discover your way out again

© DANNY YE / SHUTTERSTOCK

admission charges. These include the Hedge Maze, where motion sensors cause flowers to pop out from the neatly clipped leafy walls; a Petal Garden with a kaleidoscopic array of seasonal blooms from around the world; and a topiary walk including orangutans made from coconut fibres, a peacock whose feathered tail is an array of orchids, and a pink flower elephant spouting water from its trunk into a pool. It's all a social media sharing sensation and as 21st century a style of garden as you could imagine.

Don't Miss

→ **Walking the calming trails of the Forest Valley**

→ **Weaving your way through Singapore's largest hedge maze**

→ **Feeling the cooling spray from the world's tallest indoor waterfall**

Find Your Joy

Getting there
Jewel is connected to the arrivals hall of Singapore's Changi Airport Terminal 1, and to Terminals 2 and 3 by link bridges.

The Singapore metro connects it to the city.

Accessibility
The airport is well designed for those with limited mobility. There are wheelchair-friendly trails and an accessible-route navigation guide is available on the iChangi App.

When to go
Being an indoor climate-controlled garden, any time of year is good to visit. Around festive seasons, such as Christmas and Chinese New Year (end of January/ early February), as well as the June holiday, there are special themed displays and extra activities throughout the mall.

Further information
• Free general admission; some specific attractions charge.
• Open year-round.
• No dogs allowed except guide dogs and pets travelling with passengers.
• Over 100 places to eat and drink.
• www.jewelchangi airport.com

Other Singapore Gardens

Singapore Botanic Gardens

This botanic wonderland, a Unesco World Heritage Site, was established in 1860 and is peppered with glassy lakes, rolling lawns and themed sections, such as the Ginger Garden, with over 250 members of the Zingiberaceae family. There's also a precious patch of dense primeval rainforest with over 300 species of vegetation, half of which are now considered rare in Singapore.

Don't miss

The National Orchid Garden, the world's largest showcase of tropical orchids

Gardens by the Bay

A futuristic fantasyland of bio-domes, viewing platforms and whimsical sculptures, Gardens by the Bay is an ambitious masterpiece of urban planning that is as appealing to architecture buffs as it is to nature lovers. Housing 226,000 plants from 800 species, the Gardens' asymmetrical conservatories – the Flower Dome and Cloud Forest– rise like giant paper nautilus shells beside Singapore's Marina Bay.

Don't miss

The 164ft-tall (50m) metal and concrete Supertrees clad with over 162,900 plants

© TAKASHI IMAGES / SHUTTERSTOCK

Stroll through one of Japan's most famous gardens

JAPAN

 Design, peacefulness, views

 Early May or early November

The relaxing sound of splashing water beckons you through Renchi-mon, the original of the five gates into Kenroku-en. Standing beside the thatch-roofed Yugao-tei teahouse, your gaze will be drawn across the Hisago-ike, a pond with a gourd-like shape, to the Midori-taki, the Green Waterfall. This 21ft- (6.6m)-high cascade falls like rippling white silk amid a profusion of greenery and artfully placed rocks. It is a unique feature in such a traditional garden, and brings at once a feeling of wonder and meditative calm. This is the impressive introduction to the exquisite visual pleasures of what many consider the pinnacle of Japanese garden design.

Appreciating perfection
Begun in the early 17th century by the feudal lords of Kaga, Kenroku-en was crafted over 200 years before it opened to the public in 1871. Its name, which means 'combined six garden', refers to the sextet of attributes it perfectly embodies: seclusion; spaciousness; artificiality; antiquity; water courses; panoramas. Designed as a classical strolling garden, it has specific geographical features, including streams connecting several ponds and man-made hills planted with a rich variety of trees. A grove of over 200 plum trees (whose pink and white blossoms brighten early March), several teahouses, stone bridges and a pagoda are among the features which draw contented sighs as you progress along the gravel paths.

Right: The Green Waterfall was added to the garden in the 18th century by a Kaga *daimyō* (lord)

Below: The shapely Karasaki pine trees prepared for winter; cherry trees in blossom

© MARQUICIO PAGOLA / SHUTTERSTOCK

© SEAN PAVONE / SHUTTERSTOCK

What do you do at Kenroku-en?
I'm in charge of the maintenance and management of the garden. I've been here for 35 years.

Kenroku-en is a high maintenance garden. How big is your team?
There are seven people. Every day is a learning experience.

What's the most difficult part of the job?
There are many trees in the park, and pruning is carried out while considering the characteristics of the trees and the surrounding landscape.

Sounds tricky.
Even experienced gardeners can get confused about which branches to cut. Also, as each tree grows in a different location and environment, some trees must be worked on in contorted positions, which is a difficult task.

Hitoshi Shishime, Head of Operations

© GC PHOTOGRAPHER / SHUTTERSTOCK

© TANYA JONES / SHUTTERSTOCK

Right: Mist, and the Moon Bridge at the Portland Japanese Garden

Left: The arch of the Kotoji stone is said to resemble the bridge on a koto (Japanese zither)

Don't Miss

➔ Admiring the asymmetry of the Kotoji stone lantern

➔ Sipping tea and enjoying the view from the Sigure-tei teahouse

➔ Crossing the Hanami-bashi – the flower viewing bridge

Seasonal delights

There's something to lift the spirits whatever the time of year at Kenroku-en. In July head to Yamazaki Hill where the sunshine is filtered through the broad leaves of the horse chestnuts and maples, dappling the moss-coated ground beneath. This cool cocoon of lush greenery provides respite from the season's stifling humidity. Return in October for the same leaves to have become a dazzling display of red and gold, the ground carpeted with a mirror image of autumnal shades. And throughout the year feel calmed by the burbling water flowing down the hill into the Kasumiga-ike, the largest of the ponds.

Reflections in the water

This pond, at the heart of Kenroku-en, is where you'll find two of the garden's most iconic sights. Balanced with one long leg in the water and a shorter one on land is the Kotoji stone lantern. Be beguiled by its reflection in the pond as you look towards Uchihashi-tei, a teahouse partly suspended by stone pillars so that it seems to be floating.

Spreading their branches over Kasumiga-ike are the beautiful Karasaki pine trees, carefully tended by generations of gardeners to achieve a miraculous shape. From early November to late March, cone shaped tepees of ropes protect these historic pines from snow. Known as *yukizuri*, these ropes become part of the garden design and look especially dramatic when glistening white with snowflakes.

Find Your Joy

Getting there
Kenroku-en is in the city of Kanazawa. The garden is about 30 minutes on foot from Kanazawa train station. A bus would take about 17 minutes, or it's 10 minutes by taxi.

Accessibility
There are free wheelchairs available for visitors to use at the garden's entrance gates. However, the garden has many slopes and some narrow paths, so can cause difficulties for those with mobility issues.

When to go
Go in January and February for camellias; April and May for cherry blossoms and azaleas; May and June for irises; and October and November for autumn colours.

Further information
• Admission charge.
• Open year-round.
• No dogs allowed.

• The Sigure-tei teahouse serves green tea and Japanese-style sweets.
• www.pref.ishikawa.jp/siro-niwa/kenrokuen

Japanese Gardens Outside Japan

Portland Japanese Garden, USA

This verdant sanctuary was conceived as a symbol of post-WWII healing when Portland and Sapporo became sister cities in 1959, and today it's considered one of the most authentic Japanese gardens outside Japan. The grounds feature a teahouse, wooden pavilions and bridges, meandering stone paths and tumbling streams, all allowing serene contemplation.

Don't miss
Strolling the Pond Garden with koi ponds connected by a stream and the iconic Moon Bridge

Cowden Garden, Scotland

In 1908, the Scottish adventurer Ella Christie commissioned a Japanese-style garden for her home in Clackmannanshire. She hired the Japanese female gardener Taki Handa to help create Shā-raku-en, 'the place of pleasure and delight' – a stroll garden, centred around a lake, with paths that stretch across 7 acres (2.8 hectares) of Cowden Castle's grounds.

Don't miss
Carefully navigating the water-surrounded zigzag path

Plunge into Malaysia's rainforest and discover rare spices

MALAYSIA

 Jungle sounds, fragrance, inspiration

 November & December

As the bus pulls up outside the entrance, an alluring stretch of Malaysia's palm-fringed coast tempts from across the road. But a dip in the sea can wait until later – the Tropical Spice Garden beckons.

Set in a jungle valley, the garden is laid out on what was once a steep, terraced rubber plantation in the northwest of Penang island. On entering, it's wise to accept the insect repellent offered with your ticket – perhaps the first indication of what lies ahead – before making your way along the Zen-like path that follows the edge of a pond adorned with ferns, palms and blooming lotuses. Cross a fast-flowing stream with a hop and a skip on stepping stones and begin the climb

upwards into the humid heart of the garden, your anticipation and the chatter of the jungle building in volume as you go.

Secret Eden

The garden's life began in 2001, when a group of community naturalists set about reclaiming a five-acre plot of a long-abandoned rubber plantation from the jungle's embrace. They chose an area surrounding a natural basin, complete with reservoir and a stream trickling through it, and began planting over 500 tropical plants, including fragrant flowers, spices and rare herbs. This all created a magical home for the rainforest's residents – dusky leaf langurs and macaques, turtles, lizards, flamboyant birds such as the appropriately named Common

Right: The garden is a living museum of spices growing in their natural habitat

Below: The dusky leaf langur's coat turns from orange to dark brown as the animal matures; nutmeg

© REMI DELEPLANQUE / SHUTTERSTOCK

© DENYS KUTSEVALOV / SHUTTERSTOCK

Q&A

What is your role?
I have been tending the gardens since 2005 but rather than 'the gardener' I call myself a caretaker for Mother Nature, the force that always prevails in a rain forest.

Do you have a favourite flower that you planted?
I love the striking tacca, which we call Bat Lily because in bloom it resembles a flying bat.

What's the best sunset spot?
Head for the Giant Swing in what we call the Heart of the Garden, for an unforgettable view of the jungle and sea.

And your top dish in the cooking school?
That has to be spicy beef rendang, everyone should taste this local speciality.

Kenneth Khoo, Co-Owner

© ANILKUMART / SHUTTERSTOCK

flameback and Scarlet-backed flowerpecker, rare butterflies, and all manner of weird and wonderful insects. Enclosed by the impenetrable walls of the jungle, it soon became a hidden piece of aromatic paradise.

Opposite: The tree-like canopy shelter in Perdana Botanical Garden

Right: Cinnamon trees are grown for two years before the aromatic bark can be harvested

© EVELINE27 / SHUTTERSTOCK

Spice rush

Along the four spice terraces you can behold the goods that made the island famous as the 'Pearl of the Orient'. From the late 18th century, the spice trade brought incredible riches to Penang and spice farms popped up all over the island. The valuable plants sprout like precious jewels from the soil: the flashy scarlet spears of ginger; turmeric's hot pink blooms; nutmeg trees weighed down with their pendulous orange fruit. Lemongrass, allspice, pandan, galangal, clove, cinnamon and tamarind are all in attendance too, alongside the spiciest of them all, black pepper. In the morning or after rain, the air tingles with their scent.

Taste and learn

These are the ingredients that make Malaysian cuisine so unique and world-beatingly delicious, and in the garden's cooking school you can learn how the plants find their way into the country's signature dishes. As you pound, crush and grate each piece of bark, seed, leaf or root, the rich and familiar fragrances fill the air, and Malaysia's natural and cultural history becomes embedded in your soul. It's a full-on sensory experience, ending in the best way possible – with a delicious beef rendang.

Don't Miss

→ **Taking a fragrant stroll along the spice terraces**

→ **Dipping your feet in the bamboo garden's natural fish spa**

→ **Sipping fresh herbal tea in the garden cafe**

Find Your Joy

Getting there
The garden is a 12-mile (20km) drive from Penang's capital city, George Town. The garden has its own stop on the 101 bus route, which takes around 1 hour.

Accessibility
With steps and staircases throughout the gardens, mobility is not easy, meaning wheelchair access is limited to the main pathway, an uphill route where visitors make a U-turn at the top before descending the same path to exit.

When to go
November and December are perfect, cooler months with breezy afternoons. January and February can be very hot, while outdoor garden walks in September and October are not so easy as this is usually the wet monsoon time.

Further information
• Admission charge, includes free audio guide.
• Open year-round.
• Dogs welcome on a lead.
• Flora Cafe is housed in a wooden stilt house with a terrace.
• www.tropicalspice garden.com

Other Malaysian Tropical Gardens

Penang Botanic Gardens

Since their founding almost 140 years ago, these gardens have metamorphosed from commercial spice gardens into a centre for botanical studies, and now a beloved green lung of George Town. A mix of lakes, fountains, formal gardens and rainforest trails, the gardens make a great day out for hiking, picnics, and monkey-spotting.

Don't miss

Smelling the blooms in the orchidarium

Perdana Botanical Garden

This sprawling space in the heart of Kuala Lumpur is still known to locals by its name of Lake Gardens, given when it was created in 1888. Surrounded by skyscrapers, it's now a formal botanical garden, with tropical rainforest vegetation, pergolas filled with herbs and spices, and the spectacular Hibiscus Garden, dedicated to Malaysia's national flower, the Bunga Raya.

Don't miss

Spotting the otters in the lake

© GWOEII / SHUTTERSTOCK

Find serenity in the city at Nan Lian

 Tranquillity, bonsai, tea

 November

CHINA

Technically you're in Kowloon, one of the busiest, most densely populated places on Earth, a swirling tempest of neon signs, bubble tea shops, office towers and street markets. But inside the walls of Nan Lian Garden, you're back in the Tang Dynasty. Ok, so the visitors with selfie sticks make it clear it's not 900 CE. Still, the immaculate hedgerows, tranquil koi ponds and pine-shaded paths make it feel like you've entered another world.

This is all by design. Nan Lian, opened in 2006 on the grounds of the Chi Lin Buddhist nunnery, is a classical Chinese garden, designed in the style popularised during the Tang Dynasty (618-907 CE). Every component is carefully planned following ancient principles. The result is harmonious and deeply relaxing.

The elements of style
Like all classical Chinese gardens, Nan Lian includes four key elements: plants; rocks; water; architecture. Visitors enter at the main gate and set off on the brick path in a counterclockwise direction. This route takes you past ponds and aesthetically arranged boulders, beneath banyan trees and Japanese black pines, alongside a waterfall and hillocks planted with meticulously pruned shrubs. The main architectural element is the lotus pond's Pavilion of Absolute Perfection, an octagonal pagoda surrounded by eight Buddhist pines and linked to the land by bright orange bridges. There's also a fake mill with a wooden waterwheel, a popular photo

Right: Water features and wooden buildings are characteristic of Tang Dynasty garden design

Below: Chi Lin Nunnery is the world's largest handmade wooden building; the lotus pond

© DNDAVIS / SHUTTERSTOCK

My Garden Joy

The first time I came to Nan Lian I was new to Hong Kong and overwhelmed by the noise and lights. Though ringed by tall buildings and a busy highway, the garden provided a refuge, a slice of welcome greenery amid the urban chaos. The next time I went was the day I discovered I was pregnant with my first son. I imagined standing next to the waterfall with a baby in my arms. 'Look!' I'd say, pointing at the creamy pink lotuses floating in the pond, 'Flowers!' The last time I visited Nan Lian I had two young boys. I sat on a stone bench beneath a pagoda tree while they moved pebbles back and forth on the path, creating their own tiny magical landscapes within the larger one.

Emily Matchar

© LKUNL / SHUTTERSTOCK

© HYEONMIN LEE / SHUTTERSTOCK

© GUOZHONGHUA / SHUTTERSTOCK

Right: Victoria Peak Garden, a green oasis in the mountain above Hong Kong

Left: Calm in the concrete jungle: the Pavilion of Absolute Perfection

the rocks planted throughout the landscape are considered the bones of the garden, the structure upon which the flora can flourish. Near the Rockery are rows of bonsais, trees that have been fastidiously trimmed and trained over the years into sculptures.

Tea and harmony

At Song Cha Xie, the teahouse on the north side, guests slip off their shoes and sit at wooden tables to sip wuyi and pu'er teas prepared by the garden's tea masters. Wuyi, grown high in the mountains of Fujian province, has a deep, mineral flavour, with hints of incense and fruit. Pu'er, from Yunnan, is a fermented tea that often has an earthy undertone. Waitstaff show newbies how to brew and pour their own tea, then leave them to sip in silence.

Afterwards, stepping back out into the sunshine and seeing the skyscrapers looming above the garden walls is a bit of a shock. It's still the 21st century after all.

Don't Miss

→ Taking a photo in front of the waterfall – alongside everyone else

→ Sipping a quiet cup of pu'er tea at Song Cha Xie

→ Gawking at exquisite bonsai

spot. Every turn brings a new vista – the pagoda framed by the branches of pine trees, a pair of symmetrical bushes casting twin shadows onto a wall. The precision and artistry are somehow deeply satisfying.

Rocking out

Rocks are not an afterthought in a Chinese garden. A beautiful stone is considered just as worthy as an orchid. One of the garden's wooden halls contains the Rockery, where ancient sedimentary stones are displayed like artwork. Outside,

Find Your Joy

Getting there
Nan Lian is in Kowloon's Diamond Hill neighbourhood. The MTR train stop is Diamond Hill; the garden is a short, well-

signposted walk from exit C2.

Accessibility
Bar a few locations, most of the garden is wheelchair accessible. The garden path is paved and there are ramps to accessible bathrooms.

When to go
Hong Kong's mild climate means the gardens bloom

year-round. May through September, however, is often brutally hot, which can make outdoor strolling less pleasant. The most reliably sunny and temperate months are November to February.

Further information
• Free admission.
• Open year-round.
• No dogs allowed.
• Vegetarian cafe and a

tea shop on site.
• www.lcsd.gov.hk/en/parks/nl

Other Hong Kong Gardens

Victoria Peak Garden

Little-known even to locals, this garden is found atop the main mountain on Hong Kong Island, reached via a dizzying drive or a steep walk. Once here, you'll think you're in Victorian England: wide lawns; wrought iron gazebos; tidy rose bushes. It's a perfect spot for picnics, photos and lazy afternoons with a book. If fog settles in, as often happens, it's the most romantically spooky setting imaginable.

Don't miss

Snapping some pics by the photogenic gazebo in the rose garden

Kadoorie Farm & Botanic Garden

In the hills of Hong Kong's New Territories, Kadoorie is a teaching and research site – and a popular day trip for the public. Walking trails and stone steps wander past terraced gardens and through replanted native forest. There are organic vegetable plots, rare orchids and animal habitats designed for threatened Chinese species. Hike for hours, see the butterflies and grab some organic eggs at the shop.

Don't miss

Joining a guided tour to learn about local flora and fauna

Connect with nature in a forest garden

JAPAN

♡ Relaxation, wildflowers, walks

🕐 July

It's late July in the Tokachi Millennium Forest on Hokkaidō, and according to the poetic 72 micro-seasons into which the Japanese year is divided, this is when 'Paulownia trees produce seeds'. In Tokachi's Meadow Garden, it's also the moment when drifts of lofty giant scabious form an avenue either side of the boardwalk path. Butterflies adore these pale-yellow flowers, and occasion delight as visitors walk by and a cloud of fluttering wings takes to the air.

This large, ambitious park on Japan's northernmost main island was the idea of media tycoon Mitsushige Hayashi who wanted to offset the carbon footprint of his newspaper business, as well as create a landscape that would be sustainable for a

thousand years. In the foothills of Hokkaidō's central Hidaka Mountain range, Hayashi began by establishing a new forest of white birch, oak and magnolia.

In 2000, British garden designer Dan Pearson was commissioned to work alongside Japanese landscape designer Fumiaki Takano on a masterplan for the forest, its gardens and a working farm. The result, a triumph of naturalistic gardening, was praised by the British Society of Garden Designers as 'the best example of garden design in the 21st century.'

Drawn into the landscape

One of Pearson's masterstrokes was to sculpt a flat field in front of Tokachi's restaurant into the Earth Garden, a

© DANUTA / SHUTTERSTOCK

Right: Wild by design – pollinators frequent the Meadow Garden

Below: The Rose Garden sits in the shadow of the misty Hidaka mountains; the Kitchen Garden

Q&A

Prior to designing Tokachi Millennium Forest what was your experience of Japan?
I'd worked on projects in Tokyo, but had no experience of working in the Japanese landscape nor had I been to Hokkaidō.

So it was a leap of faith?
I could not have created this garden without the involvement of Head Gardener, Midori Shintani. The Meadow Garden, for example, is a continually evolving, living thing which requires sensitive handling. Midori is completely in tune with its rhythms and has been instrumental in its success.

What did you learn from the project?
That a garden connects people more deeply with nature and helps them appreciate its value. It's a practical solution to telling the story of good stewardship, but it also works most effectively on an emotional level to capture people's imagination.

Dan Pearson, Garden Designer

series of wave-like earthen forms covered in lawns and tall grasses. This undulating area echoes, and draws you towards, the nearby mountains. It's a perfect example of *shakkei*, an age-old feature of Japanese garden design in which the gardener 'borrows' distant scenery and makes it work in harmony with the foreground.

Spring in the forest

The Tokachi Millennium Forest is closed for six months of year, lying dormant under a thick blanket of snow. But when spring arrives in late April, the forest opens to the public and it's time to explore its Forest Garden and watch the fresh growth pushing through the ground. Buttery yellow marsh marigolds, pink and white anemone and Japanese primrose are among the flowers to be enjoyed as the frosts abate.

The natural eco-system and seasonal layering of woodland plants are the inspiration for the more ornamental Meadow

Opposite: The Lurie Garden is a rooftop garden, constructed over parking garages

Right: Boardwalks invite immersion into drifts of wildflowers and grasses

© KIICHI NORO / TOKACHI MILLENNIUM FOREST

Garden. Here there's a sense of grandeur as you wander through swathes of perennials, native species mingled with Western plants. Divided into blocks of colour – hot pinks and reds, various shades of yellow – the flowers are separated by bands of golden feather reed-grass.

At Tokachi, you can also enjoy fragrant blooms in the Rose Garden and fruit, vegetables and cut flowers in the Kitchen Garden. A table displays whatever is at its best in the current micro-season, from sunflowers and dahlias to pumpkins and dried grasses.

Don't Miss

→ **Joining a Segway guided tour of the forest**

→ **Discovering art works including pieces by Yoko Ono**

→ **Tasting produce from the Kitchen Garden**

Find Your Joy

Getting there

From Hokkaidō's Tokachi-Obihiro airport, the garden is a 1-hour drive. From the nearest train station at Tokachi

Shimizu it's a 15-minute taxi journey.

Accessibility

Wheelchairs are available for visitors. There are also accessible toilets at four locations around the garden.

When to go

From early May you can enjoy spring flowers in the forest, and later in

the month the cherry blossom. The gardens are at their peak from early July to early September.

Further information
• Admission charge.
• Open from last week of April to mid-October.
• Dogs welcome.
• Cafe on site. At Tokachi Millennium Forest Ranran Farm visitors can learn how to make cheese

and then sample it on pizzas.
• www.tmf.jp

Other Naturalistic Gardens

Lurie Garden, USA

Piet Oudolf, high priest of naturalistic drift planting, designed this section of Chicago's Millennium Park. Enclosed on two sides by a 15ft (4.5m) hedge, the garden is a botanical tribute to Illinois' tallgrass prairie. Native plants include multi-coloured coneflowers, prairie smoke and wild indigo. A wooden footbridge over shallow water slices through the garden dividing it into 'light' and 'dark' sections.

Don't miss

Enjoying the blue and purple salvias flowing like a river through the beds in June

Wildside Garden, England

Keith Wiley's rural Devon garden is a benchmark of 'new naturalism'. Over 100,000 tonnes of soil were shifted to transform a pancake-flat orchard into a rippling wonderland of mini-hills, winding paths and water holes. The planting has created landscapes ranging from dry Mediterranean to temperate woodland and meadow, offering up erythroniums in April, wisteria in May and ox-eye daisies in July.

Don't miss

Exploring the Canyons, an area devoted to South African and Californian plants

Step into the dream of a bonafide eccentric

♡ Tropical foliage, secret spaces, eroticism

🕐 December to February

SRI LANKA

Winding pathways twist and turn between dense baffles of tropical foliage, like a game of hide and seek plucked out of a dream. Banks of philodendrons open to reveal statues of sheep outlaws and cat judges. A time-darkened mirror floats on a wall of greenery in a moss-cloaked outdoor bathroom. Welcome to Brief Garden, the personal playground of a true original.

An unconventional horticulturalist

The brains behind Brief Garden, Bevis Bawa – the older brother of Sri Lanka's national architect, Geoffrey Bawa – trained as a rubber planter and advanced through the ranks of the Sri Lankan army before bucking convention to live a life of eccentric individuality in the company of artists, writers and actors in the family estate at Beruwala.

He remodelled the family rubber plantation into a stunning, secluded, European-inspired garden, full of water features, shady glades, secret corners and male nudes – Bawa was openly gay, and the gardens were a private space for parties at the fringes of Sri Lankan high society.

A secretive space

To reach this 20-acre (8-hectare) garden, you must first locate a single foliage-cloaked doorway at the end of a dirt lane. It opens to reveal a secret glade daubed in infinite shades of green, with bacchanalian sculptures popping up unexpectedly in hidden nooks – some clearly pleased to see you. It all feels tantalisingly invitation-only.

Right: A statue of the Hindu god Shiva - one of the less titillating figures at Brief Garden

Below: Seek, and ye shall find?; the garden is set on a slope, connected by concrete stairs and paths

© NIGEL JARVIS / SHUTTERSTOCK

Q&A

What makes Brief Garden special?
It's a garden full of vistas and surprises, almost like a European garden set in Sri Lanka. Bevis was heavily influenced by his travels to the West – he also created a Japanese garden after his travels to the Far East.

Lucky Bevis. Enough about him, what feeling do you get from the garden?
Brief Garden is very lush and tropical – it's heavenly. When I spend time in the garden, I feel light, free-spirited and stress-free.

My pulse is slowing already. How did you end up working at Brief Garden?
The garden and bungalow were left to my father who was Bevis Bawa's estate manager and also a landscape gardener. The rest of the staff were also given a house outside the main property at the edge of the estate, so the garden is kept in pristine condition.

Dan de Silva, Design Head

© SARAFALLSTROM / SHUTTERSTOCK

© RANJANA PERERA / SHUTTERSTOCK

Right: The Garden of Dreams was brought back to life in 2007

Left: Bevis Bawa hosted actors and artists in his characterful home

© NIGEL JARVIS / SHUTTERSTOCK

horticultural daydream. Over the decades, Brief Garden hosted everyone from actors Sir Lawrence Olivier, Vivien Leigh, Gregory Peck and Peter Finch to Agatha Christie, Aldous Huxley and Queen Ingrid of Denmark, alongside the great and good of Sri Lankan high society.

Bawa worked on the garden continuously until his death in 1992, leaving the estate to his staff in his will. Work continues daily to keep Bawa's vision alive – beds and banks are lovingly tended, gravel pathways are patiently raked, and sculptures are regularly excavated from their coverings of tropical moss.

You can wander the gardens freely, but a guide will steer you through the house, with its stacked bookshelves, homoerotic art and handmade furniture. As you explore, you may get the feeling that Bawa is still somewhere about the place and might pop back any minute to prepare for the next soiree.

Don't Miss

→ Peeking at the provocative sculptures

→ Admiring the Chinese-style moon gate

→ Listening to cascading ponds studded with lilies descending from the Bawa bungalow

Watered abundantly by the monsoons, screens of heliconias, aspidistras and philodendrons hide one area of the garden from the next, filling each turn with surprises. Leaves part to reveal hidden vistas, grotesque masks leer through the undergrowth, and in the outdoor bathroom, a male nude stands guard with a thatch of fern frond pubic hair. Unconventional is the word!

A playground for socialites

Bevis Bawa was known as a captivating host, and he invited many famous guests into his

Find Your Joy

Getting there
Getting to Brief Garden involves following a complicated series of twists and turns from Aluthgama police station

near Bentota. Coming with a car and driver is the easiest option.

Accessibility
With its steps, inclines and gravel paths, Brief Garden is not suitable for wheelchairs, but hotels in Bentota can arrange guides to assist visitors with other mobility issues through the gardens.

When to go
Come immediately after the rains to see Brief Garden at its best. Southwest Sri Lanka is lashed by rain from May to November, ensuring the gardens are lush and green come December.

Further information
• Admission charge.
• Open daily, year-round.
• No dogs allowed.

• No cafe, but meals and refreshments can be arranged with advance notice.
• www.briefgarden.com

Other Personal Gardens

Ruth Bancroft Garden & Nursery, USA

Every good garden should be a labour of love, and the dry garden created by Ruth Bancroft on this arid estate near San Francisco fits the bill. After pear and walnut plantations failed, the estate was replanted with an explosion of succulents and cacti, creating one of America's most remarkable drought-tolerant gardens.

Don't miss

Beholding the aloes in flower from January to March

Garden of Dreams, Nepal

During Nepal's early 20th-century love affair with all things European, Field Marshall Kaiser Shamsher surrounded his palace with an English-inspired garden of urns, statues, ponds, pergolas and pavilions. Over time, it fell into picturesque ruin, and was almost lost to the bulldozers before being rescued with funding from the Austrian government.

Don't miss

Sitting in the sun on the lawn, shielded from the chaos of downtown Kathmandu

Europe

Frolic among the fountains at the Villa d'Este

 Water features, amazement, views

 May

ITALY

Artists through the centuries have been inspired by the beauty of this Italian Renaissance garden – Fragonard, Corot and Turner painted or drew it, Sassoon wrote a poem in its honour, and the tinkling sounds of its fountains and waterfalls inspired Liszt to compose three famous works for piano. These and other creations pay testament to the fact that this World Heritage–listed 16th-century garden evokes a beauty that makes the spirit soar.

Grandiose plans

After Cardinal Ippolito II d'Este failed in his bid to become Pope in 1549, he relocated from Rome to the small town of Tivoli to take up an appointment as governor. Finding himself in this somewhat ignominious position, Ippolito decided to occupy himself with an ambitious project, one so magnificent that all who beheld it would marvel at the sheer audacity of his vision. Papal architect and lover of Roman antiquity, Pirro Ligorio, was appointed to take care of the garden's design. And so it was that the awe-inspiring garden at the Villa d'Este came into existence.

Visiting today, it's impossible not to feel a jolt of amazement when the steep terraces and multitudinous water features are first beheld. A feeling of enchantment soon follows, prompted by the sprays of water spangling in the sunlight and the melodic murmuring of the water rippling along the Avenue of the Hundred Fountains.

Right: Ippolito obtained statuary for his garden from the ruins of Emperor Hadrian's villa

Below: Villa d'Este had a huge effect on garden design in Europe; a fountain amid the greenery

Q&A

Renaissance gardens. Tell us why they're such a big deal in Italy.
The Renaissance started in Italy and it therefore has the largest number of gardens of that period. Many monumental gardens of that era belong to the Italian State and are open to visitors.

And what makes these gardens so extraordinary?
Formal Italian-style gardens, such as the Villa d'Este, were often created to express man's control over nature. They were also used to show off power and wealth, so are designed to impress. Statues, geometrical parterres, labyrinths and grottoes are the main elements that make up an overall theatrical effect.

So, it's worth making the trek from Rome to visit Villa d'Este?
Yes! This is one of the finest gardens in the world and one of the most important in the history of Italian gardens.

Judith Wade, CEO, Grandi Giardini Italiani

Villa d'Este

© VOLODYMYR NIK / SHUTTERSTOCK

Engineering marvel

The statistics are mind-boggling. The gardens feature over 50 fountains, 64 waterfalls and hundreds of spouts, jets and basins. Working with a hydraulic engineer, Ligorio brought in earth to create terraces and even had an aqueduct constructed. When it became apparent this wouldn't provide enough water to meet his client's demands, he requested that a tributary of the River Aniene be diverted and channelled into the garden. Natural pressure from the river forced jets of water to spurt (40ft) 12m into the air from fountains and even powered the mechanism of the 144-pipe instrument in the Fountain of the Organ, a technological marvel that still plays today. Ligorio's major achievement was to conceal all of the technology he used, so that the water moves here as if designed to do so by nature, an illusion as clever as it is magical.

Opposite: The Pope has had a private garden on Vatican Hill since medieval times

Right: The Avenue of the Hundred Fountains contains nearly 300 spouts

Whimsical features

It's not all about water, though. Classical statuary is dotted across the terraces, mostly incorporated into fountains. Greek and Roman gods are portrayed, as are dragons, dolphins, sphinxes and lions. Pegasus takes flight above a fountain, and a carved eagle – used in the arms of the Este family – casts his beady eyes over all the action. Exploring the gardens is exciting because its features are often unexpected – children, in particular, approach it as a glorious treasure hunt, with surprises on every terrace.

Don't Miss

→ Hearing the water organ play

→ Walking the length of the Avenue of the Hundred Fountains

→ Spotting Romulus and Remus at the Fountain of Rometta

Find Your Joy

Getting there
Tivoli is 30km east of Rome. Cotral buses travel to Tivoli from Rome's Ponte Mammolo metro station and regional trains depart from Stazione Tiburtina. The bus is the fastest and most convenient option, as its final stop is close to the villa.

Accessibility
A lift can take visitors from street level to the upper terrace of the garden, from where the lower terraces can be viewed. Electric vehicles are available for people with mobility issues.

When to go
The most colourful month to visit is May, when the roses and wisteria bloom. Water mist from the garden's myriad fountains makes this a delightfully cool retreat in June to August, but it can be very cold here December to February.

Further information
• Admission charge.
• Open Tuesday to Sunday, year-round.
• Dogs welcome on a lead.
• No cafe/restaurant on-site
• www.grandigiardini.it

Other Nearby Gardens

Giardini di Villa Barberini

Perched high in the Alban Hills south of Rome, the Pope's summer retreat occupies a site that was once home to a palace built for the Emperor Domitian. The 17th-century gardens incorporate archaeological remains as well as many ancient holm oaks and umbrella pines. Later additions include parterres planted with colourful annuals and the Garden of Mirrors.

Don't miss

Playing hide and seek in the maze

Vatican Gardens

Long a secret space within Vatican City, the Pope's private gardens have been open to the public since 2014. The oldest botanical garden in Italy, with plants from Mediterranean countries as well as exotic species, the gardens incorporate a picturesque villa designed by Pirro Ligorio, fountains, sculptures and archaeological remains.

Don't miss

Marvelling at the manicured hedges in the Italian Garden

Discover Arctic colour in the world's northernmost botanic garden

♡ Alpine plants, fjord views, wonderment

🕐 Mid-June to mid-July

NORWAY

The Arctic Circle is not an easy place to be a plant. For three months of the winter, the sun never peeks over the horizon. For three more in summer, it forgets to set, causing havoc with nature's circadian rhythms. Any plant foolhardy enough to attempt to grow here must cope with some of Earth's most extreme climates. That's why most don't even try.

Except in Tromsø's Botanic Garden, that is. Located 217 miles (350km) above the Arctic Circle at 69.6942°N, this northern oasis exists at a latitude that would have most sensible plants shrivelling at their roots. It's 714 miles (1149km) north of Oslo, and cloaked in snow for much of the year – and yet the garden offers a profusion of floral colour more reminiscent of a midsummer's day.

The experience is as awe-inspiring as it is bewildering.

Uncanny splendour

Rhododendrons sprawl over rocky slopes. Delicate primulas, gentians and auriculas sprout among rocky boulders. Buttercups, anemones, windflowers and saxifrages bloom until the first snows arrive in October. Wandering the garden's hillside paths is a disorientating experience: one minute, you're looking at a neatly tended rockery bursting with crimson, yellow, tangerine, and cornflower blues; the next you're gazing over a frosty fjord towards the distant shapes of the Lyngen Alps.

It takes careful horticultural cultivation to maintain a garden this far north. Plants have been selected for their hardiness from all around the globe: the Himalayas, the Andes, New Zealand, the

Right: Large-scale rockeries provide a suitable home for plants from mountain regions

Below: The Arctic summer provides an intense growing period; the delicate nomocharis

© ARTEM NEDOLUZHKO / SHUTTERSTOCK

© KRISTIAN NYVOLL / THE ARCTIC-ALPINE BOTANIC GARDEN

Q&A

What makes the garden unique?
Our plants are specialists in coping with climatic extremes. I think it's special that here in the high north you can enjoy rare plants collected from the rooftops of the world – from the Andes to the Himalayas!

You must need super-green fingers to get plants to grow this far north.
Alpines are specialists in making the most of warmth and sunlight when it comes, and in midsummer they take off like a rocket. In fact, we worry when it's too warm and sunny, as they grow too fast!

A gardener who worries about sunlight – that's a first.
Yes. I'm definitely the opposite to most gardeners in that respect.

Top tip?
I love walking through the garden at 1 or 2am in summer, when the midnight sun creates strange shadows, patterns and colours. It's a unique experience. Especially when you've had a few beers.

Kristian Nyvoll, Scientific Adviser & Head Gardener

© KRISTIAN NYVOLL / THE ARCTIC-ALPINE BOTANIC GARDEN

Right: Take in the Botanical Garden Copenhagen from the terrace of the Palm House

Left: Primulas peep out towards the snow-capped Lyngen Alps

Indigenous people, the Sámi, and to the Vikings too, both of whom used Norway's native plants for traditional medicines and folk remedies. It's a cross between a suburban rockery, a science lab, a herb garden and a history lesson, all rolled into one.

An Arctic oasis

Since it opened in 1994, the Botanic Garden has become a much-loved Tromsø landmark. In summer, townsfolk wander the paths, have picnics, or stop for coffee and waffles at Hansine Hansen's cosy timber-clad cafe. In winter, when snow and ice cloak the ground, the garden's hilltop location offers fabulous, wintry views over the surrounding fjords .

And if you're lucky enough to visit on a really dark, clear night, you might even be treated to a display by the Northern Lights: glimpsed under the aurora's flickering, sparkling light stream, this scientific garden transforms into something out of a fairy tale.

Don't Miss

→ Seeking out the super-rare Himalayan blue poppy

→ Enjoying waffles and cloudberry jam at Hansine Hansen's cafe

→ Walking in winter to see the Northern Lights

Falkland Islands, Tajikistan, Taiwan, Morocco, Afghanistan, Lesotho, Mexico. In fact, it's said there's a plant from every continent here – including the garden's showpiece specimen, the rare Himalayan blue poppy and the world's largest collection of gentian. It's one of the few gardens on Earth where the world's northernmost and southernmost plants bloom alongside one another.

Not all the plants are so exotic, however. Hardy herbs like sage, rosemary, dill and alliums and old perennials also feature, providing a link in time to Norway's

Find Your Joy

Getting there
Tromsø has direct flights from Oslo and major European cities. You can also arrive aboard the Hurtigruten ferry.

The gardens are on the northern edge of Tromsø, about 2.5 miles (4km) north of the centre and the harbour. Several public buses stop nearby.

Accessibility
The Botanic Garden is located on a steep hillside above the town, but its paths are well maintained and readily accessible to people of reduced

mobility and wheelchair users. It is free to visit, and there are no gates, meaning it can be visited at any time of day.

When to go
The garden shows off its best colours in midsummer (mid-June to mid-July), but spring (March to May) and autumn (September to November) are very

pleasant too. For the Northern Lights, November to February is peak aurora season.

Further information
• Free admission.
• Open year-round.
• Dogs welcome.
• Cafe on-site.
• www.visittromso.no/arctic-alpine-botanic-garden

Other Great Scandinavian Gardens

Botanical Garden Copenhagen, Denmark

While most visitors head for the funfair rides of Tivoli, plant nerds make a beeline for Copenhagen's botanical garden – an oasis right in the heart of the city. It's home to Denmark's largest collection of plants – 13,000 in all, from rare trees to rhododendrons, wildflowers and mountain plants. The garden's 27 glasshouses are stunning: the centrepiece is the 1874 Palm House.

Don't miss
Watching the colourful residents of the garden's butterfly house

Gunnebo Garden, Sweden

This delightful manor garden 9 miles (15km) south of Gothenburg presents a snapshot of the great age of Swedish gardens during the 18th century. Attached to the eponymous Gunnebo House, it's actually three gardens in one: a formal garden, a sprawling, English-style landscaped park and a working kitchen garden, which specialises in growing heirloom fruit and vegetables.

Don't miss
Lunching at the manor's organic cafe, Kaffehus och Krog

The Joy of Exploring Gardens **153**

Follow your nose through a perfume garden

♡   Olfaction, flower power, rapture

🕐   April to June

FRANCE

Walking through the meadows of pink, white and red rose blooms in May at Les Jardins du Musée International de la Parfumerie is joy on acid. The fresh, green, honey scent of the centifolia roses is powerful and intoxicating. Delicate petals, miraculously arranged by nature into sturdy cups, conjure up images of ladies in hats hobnobbing over afternoon tea or 18th-century still life masters bent over easels, or young literary heroines flouncing through fields. The perfume's sensual elegance, natural grace and period romance make the heart sing. Little wonder then that the centifolia rose has long been the most precious muse for the famous perfumers of this part of southern France.

Find your nose

Designed in 2010, the gardens form part of the International Museum of Perfumery (MIP), located in the nearby Provençal town of Grasse. They showcase flowers and plants which have been used in the town's perfume industry since the 16th century when local tanner Galimard ingeniously scented a pair of gloves to disguise the unpleasant stench of leather. By the early 1900s Grasse was the world's largest producer of perfumery's raw materials, and the gardens – covering 6 acres (2.4 hectares) of agricultural land around a canal in Mouans-Sartoux, southeast of the town – are a dazzling potpourri of those flowers that make Grasse essences so revered. As you walk around, every bloom, bush, aromatic herb and tree – 800 species in all – can be touched, rubbed

Right: Alongside flowers, the garden is planted with the traditional trees of Grasse

Below: Roses – for centuries a major player in the French perfume industry; a field of poppies

Q&A

What's the garden's most surprising aspect?
The fact that perfume plants are found alongside natural spontaneous vegetation, resulting in a country garden that's sometimes punk, sometimes chic.

Favourite moments?
A walk through the rose field in May when several thousand rose bushes flower. Or inhaling the refreshing fragrance of the small labyrinth of vetiver trees, patchouli, pepper trees and chillies.

Something unexpected?
Crumple the foliage of *Melianthus major* (honey bush) and it exudes a peanut smell mixed with popcorn. Find it in the shade of the faux-acacias (black locust) just before the Olfactory Trail.

Favourite scent?
Roses. It's magical discovering and rediscovering the huge variety of scents.

Christophe Mège, Head Gardener

and sniffed, creating olfactory acrobatics in spades.

The smell of haute couture

Show fields of jasmine, rose, tuberose, violet and mimosa transport visitors to a bygone era when flower fields carpeted a vast area around Grasse. Haute-couture fashion houses such as Christian Dior and Chanel still extract essences for their luxury perfumes from the centifolia roses and jasmine cultivated on third-generation farms here. But industrialisation and the growth of synthetic scents in perfumery have whittled the region's flower fields down to 100 acres (40 hectares) today.

Celebrating savoir-faire

In the landscaped garden, don't miss the visual details honouring local heritage and savoir-faire: the rose-smothered metal-and-wickerwork pergola evokes the baskets of flower harvesters who still pick 16,000-plus flowers

Opposite: Botany with a view at the Flore-Alpe mountain garden

Right: Jasmine was once used by the tanners of Grasse to perfume leather

© CARLO BARBIERO / MUSÉES DE GRASSE

a day; the wooden pergola is reminiscent of the huts where kilo after kilo of pearly white jasmine flowers are traditionally dried. Along the Parcours Olfactif (Olfactory Trail), arranged by olfactory family, inhale deeply to savour the luxuriant cocktail of scents with citrus, woody, floral, fruity, musky, amber and spicy notes. Revel in fresh, revitalising herbaceous notes in the aromatics section where varietals of sage, thyme, mint, fennel, rosemary and more provide a sense of stillness, serenity and the *joie de vivre* of summer holidays in Provence.

Don't Miss

→ **Smelling lavender – a quintessential perfume of Provence**

→ **Learning about specific flowers on themed open days**

→ **Creating your own perfume at Grasse's Musée International de la Parfumerie**

Find Your Joy

Getting there
Mouans-Sartoux train station, with services to Grasse (7 minutes) and along the coast to Cannes (20 minutes) and Nice

(one hour), is a 15-minute walk north along Chemin des Gourettes. Bus 20 links Grasse bus station with the 'Les Jardins du MIP' bus stop. Motorists can find free parking next to the garden.

Accessibility
Most of the landscaped garden is wheelchair-accessible. Shaded picnic tables, benches

and deckchairs beneath cypress, fig and almond trees or creeper-clad pergolas are plentiful.

When to go
The garden's field of centifolia roses is at its finest late April to early June. Jasmine, violets, tuberose, orange blossom and serried rows of purple lavender flower at this time too.

Further information
• Admission charge (half price with a ticket for Grasse's perfumery museum).
• Open April to November.
• Dogs welcome on a lead.
• Cafe on site.
• www.museesde grasse.com/jmip/ presentation

Other Fragrance Gardens

Flore-Alpe, Switzerland

It's in June and July that this 1920s alpine garden, arranged around traditional Heidi-esque wooden chalets high in the Valais region, blazes a rainbow of colour and scent. Stone-flag paths, footbridges across streams, and rocky moraine beds polka-dotted with hardy rock jasmine inject story-book charm into its prized botanical collection of alpine flora.

Don't miss

Visiting in May when pink and white rhododendrons are at their most fragrant

Le Jardin des Arômes, France

In addition to its celebrated bounty of olives, the traditional town of Nyons in Provence has a public garden celebrating the rich aromatic heritage of France's hot south. On the banks of the River Eygues, this enchanting 'aroma garden' takes visitors past sweet-smelling lemon balm, thyme and 200 other perfumed, aromatic and medicinal plants traditionally distilled to make essential oil and floral waters (hydrosols).

Don't miss

Being delighted by glorious sunflower-yellow mimosa in January and February

Appreciate the beauty of a drought-tolerant Mediterranean garden

♡ Architecture, design, calm

🕐 April

GREECE

Golden hour in Athens. That gorgeous time as the sun slips down the sky towards the water, bathing all in a honey and caramel light. Warm sea breezes prickle your skin as you stand beneath the shady canopy of the Lighthouse atop the Stavros Niarchos Foundation Cultural Centre (SNFCC). Up here you feel like an eagle surveying the surrounding 52-acre (21-hectare) park. A broad stone path slices through an undulating sea of feathery native grasses. Further down the gently graded slope the more structural forms of shrubs and some 350 olives trees merge into the concrete edge of the city.

A roof with a view
The Lighthouse viewing platform of the SNFCC – a remarkable Renzo

Piano-designed building which houses the Greek National Opera and the National Library – also places the park in the wider landscape. There are panoramas out to the Mediterranean as well as to the iconic hills and mountains of this antique city: Mt Hymettos; Lykavittos Hill; the Acropolis. This is no accident – the SNFCC is in Kallithea, which translates as 'beautiful view', a concept whose realisation underpins the park's design.

In modern times this was once the flat landscape of a horse-racing track and, going some 2500 years further back, the original port of Athens. It is now a cultural hub and park that has been awarded LEED Platinum Certification, the highest possible rating for environmentally conscious and sustainable building projects. Irrigation is

Right: Greece's famous aromatic plants provide structure and fragrance

Below: The canopy of the Opera House represents a cloud; olive trees abound

© ANDREAS SIMOPOULOS

© YIORGIS YEROLYMBOS

Q&A

The park can look very dry and parched.
We try to educate people to understand why this is happening. The first year we had some complaints. People asked 'What are you doing? The park is dying!' The Great Lawn is planted with a type of grass that hibernates and goes yellow in the winter. So we put up some signs saying 'the lawn is sleeping, it'll get back to being green in springtime'.

What do you do with all the olives?
We harvest them in November and take them to an olive oil grinding mill. This year we had extra virgin olive oil which we donated to a homeless shelter. In the past we've used the oil to make soap, scented with some of the herbs grown in the park such as lavender and thyme.

Helli Pangalou, Landscape Architect and Co-Designer of Stavros Niarchos Park

© ANDREAS SIMOPOULOS

© ANDREAS SIMOPOULOS

Right: Queen Amalia would often tend the Athens National Garden herself

Left: A geodesic dome provides exhibition space and an angular foil to the greenery

bloom and release their potent fragrances. And when the ground is slightly damp, it is the most sensual time to slip off your shoes and follow the serpentine grass path through the Labyrinth, a garden design element inspired by classical Greek myth.

Cool off under the trees

Sage green metal chairs are scattered around the park, and visitors create an interactive choreography with these portable seats, shifting them around to the shadiest spots beneath the twisted branches of the half-century-old olive trees or the pine scented boughs of Cypresses. For those who prefer sun to shade, there's no better place than the Great Lawn. Laying back on the grass here, listen for the sound of children laughing as they create their own compositions on the playground pieces in the nearby Musical Garden. You'll soon find there is nowhere else you'd rather be.

Don't Miss

→ Finding your way to the centre of the Labyrinth

→ Breathing in the scent of lavender and other aromatic plants

→ Appreciating the park's design and views from the Lighthouse

minimal throughout the park, the water coming either from rain or bore holes. Its borders have been planted with the drought-tolerant species of flora that have naturally adapted to arid conditions of the Mediterranean.

Breath in the aromas

When it does rain in Athens (mainly in winter and spring) the air freshens and Stavros Niarchos Park comes alive. This is when the aromas of the sage, rosemary, thyme and lavender are at their sweetest. In the western section of the park, species of roses

Find Your Joy

Getting there
The park is in Kallithea, 3.5 miles (5.5km) southwest of central Athens (there's a free bus from near Syntagma Square) and a

short walk from the coast at Palaio Faliro.

Accessibility
The park has been specifically designed to be as accessible as possible to wheelchair users and those with mobility issues.

When to go
July and August for blooms of lavender; October for the olive

harvest. From June to September the park hosts many free events including music festivals. In December it is lit up for Christmas and looks very festive.

Further information
• Free admission.
• Open year-round
• Dogs welcome in the park, except for the Great Lawn, the Labyrinth and

the playgrounds.
• Cafes on site.
• www.snfcc.org/en/snfcc/stavros-niarchos-park

Other Greek Gardens

Athens National Garden

Designed by Queen Amalia in 1838, these former royal gardens are a lovely shady retreat from the heat and traffic of central Athens. Walk under the 12 slender palm trees planted by Queen Amalia herself and then check out the Judas trees, oleanders, Australian pines and century-old holm oaks.

Don't miss

The ruins of a Roman courtyard discovered during 19th-century excavations

Botanical Park & Gardens of Crete

This park, in the foothills of the White Mountains, arose from the ashes of a wildfire that destroyed some 100,000 olive trees in 2003. The Marinakis family replaced their olive grove with fruit-bearing trees, herbs, spices and medicinal and decorative plants from around the world. The result is a garden that tempts the taste buds.

Don't miss

Relaxing under spring blossoms in the cherry tree garden

Discover nature on an industrial scale

♡ Architecture, history, surprise

🕐 October

Steel magnate August Thyssen was a visionary, but even he could hardly have imagined that the iron works in northern Duisburg he opened in 1902 would be rebooted as a beloved post-industrial park and playground a century later. The belching plant in western Germany's Ruhr region – once the backbone of the country's coal and steel industry – soldiered on until the 1970s' global steel crisis ushered in its demise. On 4 April 1985 workers wiped their sweaty brows for the last time at the end of the final shift. But it wasn't the end of the plant.

It took another visionary, German landscape architect Peter Latz, to turn the silenced blast furnaces, ore bunkers and casting houses into a shining beacon of the 250-mile (400km) Industrial Heritage Trail that connects over 50 sites that shaped the region's history for 150 years. Instead of letting the plant devolve into a wasteland, Latz dreamed up the Landschaftspark Duisburg-Nord, a clunky name for a complex that's a captivating combination of history, culture and nature.

Tribute to the past

Of course, the concept of turning industrial relics into recreational spaces is hardly unique. But the Landschaftspark is different in that it embraces the site's gritty pedigree instead of erasing it, leaving its DNA intact and recasting its hulking structures in new roles. Head up the defunct blast furnace for giddying views of the park and the Ruhr. Cycle along railroad tracks once used to

Right: Plants of the post-war period adorn the industrial heritage of Landschaftspark

Below: Blast furnaces now provide views not fumes; relics are reborn

© LUDGER STAUDINGER / LANDSCHAFTSPARK DUISBURG-NORD

© HAVESEEN / SHUTTERSTOCK

Q&A

Nature and industry, isn't that a contradiction?
Not at all. Although the industrial building is the park's focal point, nature has reclaimed its place. In fact, because of the extremely diverse terrain and soils, unusual plants have developed that are only found in these types of post-industrial spaces.

Any animals?
Lots! Bats, natterjack toads, around 100 species of beetles and more than 60 species of birds live here, especially in the 'Wildnis' (wilderness) area, which was able to develop undisturbed into one of the park's richest biotopes after the steelworks closed.

Secret tip?
The views of blazing red vines on an autumn stroll along the elevated walkway above Sinter Park.

Frank Jebavy, Park Director

© HAVESEEN / SHUTTERSTOCK

© HAVESEEN / SHUTTERSTOCK

transport coal and iron. Watch daredevils rappel down Monte Thysso, the 'peak' of a storage bunker turned climbing garden. You can scuba dive amid artificial reefs and sunken wrecks in the cylindrical gas tank and catch a concert under the stars.

Opposite: Evening light show at Weltkulturerbe Völklinger Hütte

Right: An industrial wasteland has been recycled into an adventure playground

Nature in unexpected places

As for the gardens, don't come here looking for manicured lawns and formal flower beds. The natural joys of the Landschaftspark are a bit more 2.0. Little by little, nature is reclaiming the terrain. Around 450 flowering plant species now flourish here, including rare and exotic ones that arrived as stowaways on ships ferrying in iron ore and other raw materials from Africa and the Americas. Purple spurflowers push through crevices in concrete walls. White-blossom hawthorns flank bicycle paths. Water lilies thrive in cooling tanks. Bees buzz around acacia blanketing slag

heaps. And rows of poplars line a canal. In the old ore bunkers, you can sniff pink roses and magenta-hued buddleias, picnic under birch trees, chase butterflies or play hide-and-seek among the hedges.

The Landschaftspark may challenge, perhaps even redefine, our perception of natural beauty. But when the sky darkens and the light installation by British artist Jonathan Park bathes the buildings and trees in a sci-fi-esque chorus of colour, it's easy to feel the romance and healing magic of nature here.

Don't Miss

→ Climbing to the top of the blast furnace viewing platform

→ Smelling flowers growing wild in storage bunkers

→ Basking in the glow of a massive light installation

Find Your Joy

Getting there
From Duisburg's main train station, tram 903 travels directly to the 'Landschaftspark-Nord' stop. The park entrance is about a 10-minute signposted walk away.

Accessibility
The park is largely wheelchair accessible, though paths are often uneven, and assistance may be needed in some areas. Guide dogs are allowed everywhere. There are five accessible toilets on the site.

When to go
April and May are when flora and fauna wake up after the long winter: lizards scurry along railway tracks, dragonflies hatch on the canal banks, and anemones, cherries and lilies blossom. In July and August you can catch concerts or a festival and watch ducks frolic, while autumn (September/October) sees the vines

erupt in a blaze of carmine.

Further information
• Free admission.
• Open year-round.
• Dogs welcome on a lead, except in event spaces.
• Restaurant with beer garden in the former switching house.
• www.landschafts park.de

Other German Symbols of Renewal

Maximilianpark

A giant glass elephant welcomes you to Maximilian Park in Hamm. Climb its trunk for splendid views over the entire park, created on the site of an abandoned colliery in 1984. Embarking on an aimless wander takes you through themed gardens filled with herbs and roses, or a sea of perennial flower beds designed by Dutch garden architect Piet Oudolf.

Don't miss

Marvelling at butterflies in their tropical enclosure

Weltkulturerbe Völklinger Hütte

As many as 17,000 workers toiled in hellish heat and smoke at the peak of production in the hulking Völklinger Hütte ironworks in the Saar region. Since closing in 1986, it has gone from hell to heaven, with flowers, trees and mosses reclaiming vast parts of the huge complex. It was declared a Unesco World Heritage Site in 1994.

Don't miss

Heading up the 150ft-high (45m) former blast furnace for bird's-eye views

© PETER ALTMEYER / 500PX

Take a shady stroll through history at Trsteno

CROATIA

♡ Nostalgia, views, history

🕐 April

Those Tyrells, they sure loved to plot. Even the sublime sea views of their garden pavilion didn't distract them from orchestrating King Joffrey's grisly demise. If you have no idea what any of this means, fear not. Trsteno Arboretum's star turn as a location in HBO series *Game of Thrones* is by no means the most interesting thing about it. But if you're a fan, you'll be immediately transported into the fantasy world.

Summer escape
It was in 1494 that a noble from nearby Dubrovnik (then known as Ragusa) built a summer villa here and surrounded it with gardens influenced by the ideals of the Italian Renaissance. An inscription dating from 1502 sums up his philosophy: 'Visitors, behold the traces of human hands, whose excellent skills have tamed the wildness of nature.'

It's easy to see the attraction of the site. Only 11 miles (17km) from the famously beautiful walled city, the estate occupies a terrace overlooking the dazzling Adriatic with views stretching out over the Elafiti Islands. The Gučetić-Gozze family held on to the property for 450 years, developing the gardens as the centuries ticked over, until it passed into state ownership in 1945.

Green embrace
Arriving in Trsteno village, the presence of the arboretum is heralded by two vast centuries-old oriental plane trees set alongside the coastal

© NADTOCHIY / SHUTTERSTOCK

Right: Neptune's pond is home to bull frogs and goldfish

Below: A King's Landing? The garden provides a fine view of Trsteno Harbour; osteospermum and friends

© NADTOCHIY / SHUTTERSTOCK

Do you have a favourite part of the Arboretum?

I love all of it, from the historic gardens to the olive groves, to the places with natural vegetation.

Let's narrow it down. If you had to choose a favourite plant, what would it be?

One of my favourites is an old American lime tree (*Tilia americana*) which can be found near the aqueduct behind our fountain. This tree was planted in 1858 and it's now over 115ft (35m) high.

So, tall people should feel at home here. What else should visitors keep an eye out for?

Look out for our oldest trees that are growing in the northern part of the Renaissance garden (behind the fountain) but also our historic buildings: the summer villa, the pavilion with beautiful sea views, the old chapel, the fountain and the aqueduct.

Ivan Šimić, Director

© NADTOCHIY / SHUTTERSTOCK

Right: Quiet haven: the Franciscan Monastery in Dubrovnik

Left: The summer retreat was planted with seeds from ships travelling the world

© TARTANPARTY / SHUTTERSTOCK

Don't Miss

→ Gazing out to sea from the garden's edge

→ Standing in awe beneath the giant plane trees

→ Cooling off beside the fountain

highway. Entering the park on a hot summer's day, the greenery quickly swallows you up, the lofty canopy providing an escape from the unrelenting Dalmatian sun.

The path from the entrance pops you out between the sturdy stone villa and the clifftop pavilion. The exotic palms and succulents planted here are relative newcomers, a passion of one of the 19th-century Counts.

After you've absorbed the astonishing sea views, the main garden axis continues on the other side of the house, leading past a small 16th-century chapel

to an over-the-top baroque fountain. Erected in 1736 it takes the form of a nymphaeum, with a central figure of Neptune overlooking a pond, flanked by water-spouting nymphs and frolicking dolphins. It's fed by an aqueduct that continues the axis through a grove of magnificent mature trees to a creek at the top of the property. Even in this more formal part of the gardens, there's still a touch of wildness about it. It doesn't feel overly manicured.

Go west

Often overlooked, the Arboretum extends westwards to incorporate a meadow, a historic olive grove and a garden that was added in the early 20th century, with steps leading down to the cerulean sea. Dotted with statues, gazebos and terraces, with more than a hint of faded grandeur, it draws you in to a timeless Mediterranean tableau, a world away from the tourist bustle of Dubrovnik.

Find Your Joy

Getting there
Buses heading west from Dubrovnik stop at Trsteno, including Libertas Dubrovnik services 12, 15, 21, 22 and 35.

Accessibility
The only parts of the arboretum that are suitable for wheelchairs are some of the paths around the villa. Call ahead to arrange for direct vehicle access to the villa via the staff entrance.

When to go
In April the path in front of the villa is bursting with

the sights and scents of Lady Banks' roses and Chinese wisteria in bloom. The shady trails and sea breezes make it a great place for a stroll in July and August.

Further information
• Admission charge.
• Open year-round.
• No dogs allowed in the main gardens, but they are welcome in the

western section.
• No cafe on site
• www.pvdp.hr

Other Historic Dubrovnik Gardens

Lokrum Reserve

A 10-minute ferry ride from Dubrovnik's old harbour leads to this lush island, the whole of which is protected as a nature reserve. Its main hub is an 11th-century Benedictine monastery that was converted into a palace in the 19th century. The cloister and palace gardens have been partially restored, and there's a little botanic garden nearby.

Don't miss

The cypress-lined Path of Paradise leading through the centre of the island

Franciscan Monastery cloister

It may be tiny but the palm-filled Romanesque-gothic cloister garden at the centre of Dubrovnik's friary is exceptionally pretty. It was built in the 14th century as a space for peaceful contemplation and, despite the hordes of tourists, it somehow remains that way.

Don't miss

The capitals of the 120 slender double columns which surround it, each of which is carved with an image of people, plants or animals

Discover the naturalistic gardens of an outstanding plantswoman

♡ Inspiration, design, plant diversity

◷ April to June

ENGLAND

Spiky blue Mediterranean sea holly, swaying drifts of stipa grasses and lush lime green euphorbias erupt like islands out of a sea of gravel. It's a colour palette that acts like a balm to a busy mind. In June, bearded irises and Californian poppies join the party while a lofty eucalyptus stands sentinel in the background. This is the Gravel Garden, the inspiring opening act of the gardens and nursery that Beth Chatto spent decades creating.

Chatto was famous for her 'right plant, right place' approach to gardening. Way ahead of her time, she championed native plants, rejected pesticides and worked with nature rather than trying to subdue it. From 1960, she started transforming an old fruit farm around her bungalow home belonging to her husband, the botanist Andrew Chatto, by choosing the most suitable plants for the challenging conditions.

Blooming gravel

The Gravel Garden is considered Chatto's greatest triumph. In 1991, as an experiment, she dug up the garden's car park and began planting the poor, free-draining soil with drought tolerant perennials, grasses and bulbs. There has never been any irrigation yet the Gravel Garden has flourished, despite this being one of the driest parts of the UK.

Although not formally trained as a landscape gardener, Chatto was a skilled flower arranger. She loved *ikebana* and used that Japanese arrangement style of asymmetric forms to create the striking shapes of her borders. This was the inspiration

Right: Euphorbia 'Fireglow' blooms in the Water Garden

Below: A dried-up river bed inspired Chatto to plant the Gravel Garden; Mediterranean sea holly.

Q&A

What was Beth Chatto like?
The plants were her babies and she lived completely for the garden. She was also very impatient and demanding. She was still working in the garden into her 70s when I started here in 2001.

Have you been tempted to tinker with Chatto's original design?
It's not a museum, so we do bring in new plants, but they have to be in keeping. Beth really didn't like anything overbred. So no big, blousy hybrids, no weird echinacea in strange colours.

How does the garden make you feel?
If it's during work time, it can make me feel extremely stressed. I just see everything that needs doing and that hasn't been done. But if I come in late in the evening, I can enjoy the feel of it and see it with the same eyes as a visitor.

Åsa Gregers-Warg, Head Gardener

© BETH CHATTO'S PLANTS & GARDENS

for the placement of trees in the Gravel Garden where, in July, the weeping branches of the Mount Etna broom, heavy with fragrant, bright yellow blossoms, draw your eyes up to the sky.

Pools of tranquillity

The greater part of Chatto's garden is taken up with woodlands and wetland areas. The Water Garden, originally a boggy hollow, is a series of ponds surrounded by moisture-loving species such as irises, lilies and willow. There's little in the way of hard landscaping. Neatly clipped lawns run right up to the water's edge and under leafy trees where the temperature is several degrees cooler. Here you will find peace, even on the hottest of days.

Pleasure through the year

In the Woodland Garden, beneath the calming dappled light of oaks and acers, the ground sprouts with shade-loving bulbs, such as snowdrops, daffodils and crocuses

Opposite: Derek Jarman described his gravel garden as 'a therapy'

Right: Wild garlic and ferns catching the sun in the Woodland Garden

in spring. From late spring you can inspect shrubs like *Exochorda macrantha*, 'The Bride', with its delicate white racemes.

The Scree Garden is like a jewel box, with alpines such as anemones and dianthus providing pops of colour amid the lichen-spotted stones and boulders. These are gardens designed to provide pleasure throughout the year. Trees such as dawn redwoods and deciduous conifers create dramatic autumn hues, and ornamental grasses are left to sway in the breeze, lending structure and form in winter.

Don't Miss

→ Taking in the living tapestry of the Gravel Garden

→ Admiring the purple blossoms of the Judas tree in May

→ Seeking out souvenirs in the extensive nursery shop

Find Your Joy

Getting there
The gardens are in Elmstead Market, a village 5 miles (8km) east of Colchester. Colchester Town is the nearest train station, with bus connections to the village.

Accessibility
There is wheelchair and pushchair access to the gardens, and accessible toilets near the entrance. A transcript can be provided of the guided tour for the hard of hearing.

When to go
February for snowdrops; March for daffodils and hellebores; May for bearded irises in the Gravel Garden, and moisture-loving irises and candelabra primula in the Water Garden; August and September for late flowering perennials and ornamental grasses.

Further information
• Admission charge.
• Open mid-January to mid-December.
• No dogs allowed.
• Cafe on site.
• www.bethchatto. co.uk

Other English Gardens with a Chatto Connection

Great Dixter

Christopher Lloyd was a dear friend and correspondent of Chatto for many decades. He is best known for his refashioning of the beautiful Arts and Crafts garden (originally designed by Edwin Lutyens) that he inherited in the Sussex Weald. An intimate series of garden rooms include imaginatively clipped yew hedges, wildflower meadows, a sunken pool, masses of pots and mixed borders bursting with seasonal colour.

Don't miss

Being transported by the Exotic Garden's tropical flowers and foliage

Prospect Cottage

This informal garden of poppies, yellow sedum, sea kale and santolina sprouting out of inhospitable shingle was created by artist and film-maker Derek Jarman. While on an outing to Dungeness in June 1990, Chatto and Christopher Lloyd came across the pitch-black cottage and chatted to Jarman about his gardening methods and plantings. It would be one of the inspirations for Chatto's Gravel Garden.

Don't miss

Examining sculptures crafted from driftwood, shells, stones and rusting metal

© AC MANLEY / SHUTTERSTOCK

Stroll amid a symphony of plants on Ischia

ITALY

♡ Geraniums, classical music, calm

🕐 April

From the well-tended slopes of a terraced escarpment high above the Bay of Forio on the Italian island of Ischia, the sweeping view is mesmerising. The soft sparkle of the Mediterranean is complemented by the crinkled volcanic hump of Monte Epomeo and framed by the subtle shades and colours of a garden that has been called 'the most beautiful park in Italy'.

The Giardini La Mortella (Myrtle Gardens) is a mosaic of ecological diversity. Indeed, it's hard to imagine a place where such a wide variety of vegetation is crammed into just 5 acres (2 hectares). From desert agave to Asian water lilies, and from a sun-themed temple to a meditative Thai pavilion, the diversity on offer is dazzling and inspiring.

Home of the Waltons
The garden is the legacy of one married couple: British classical composer, William Walton (1902–83) and writer Susana Walton (1926–2010). Designed by master landscape architect, Russell Page in the 1950s on the Waltons' Ischia estate, La Mortella was reputedly inspired by the Moorish gardens of Spain's Alhambra.

Even the unassuming entrance is gorgeous: a mini gatehouse halfway down a walled lane, covered in climbing foliage and guarded by a quartet of carefully trimmed trees.

Once inside, the garden is split into two broad sections. The lower segment (The Valley) is humid and tropical, while the terraced upper slopes (The Hills) feature Mediterranean plants interspersed with strategic lookouts, with views to remind you that you're still in Italy.

© JUNJUN / SHUTTERSTOCK

Right: Wind chimes tinkle around the Thai pavilion in the Oriental Garden

Below: The endangered Egyptian blue water lily thrives in the pond; a sphinx in repose

© FONT83 / GETTY IMAGES

© WIRESTOCK / GETTY IMAGES

Q&A

What makes the gardens special?
The love story of William and Susana Walton, who forged the garden to create a haven where they could find inspiration and live a creative, productive life.

Aw. Can you pinpoint just one highlight?
The surprises that you find at every corner; you have to explore it, get lost in the paths and discover unexpected views and rare plants.

Unexpected views, you say. How do we know we're in Ischia?
The beautiful native Mediterranean plants play a very important role. And then of course we have the many wonderful views towards the sea and the distant village.

Sounds sublime. Any challenges?
Climate change: extremes of drought and temperatures that require us to rethink our maintenance plans, and the arrival of new foreign pests.

Alessandra Vinciguerra, Director

© CIRO ORABONA CREATIVE / SHUTTERSTOCK

The Joy of Exploring Gardens **175**

© CHRISTIAN MUERINGER / AWL IMAGES

Right: An Olympic-sized pool is one of the aquatic joys of Negombo park

Left: The garden takes advantage of its position facing the glinting Med

Don't Miss

→ Climbing to William's Rock, where the composer's ashes are buried

→ Admiring the reliefs in the Temple of the Sun

→ Attending a classical concert in the theatre

Global colours

The Valley was designed by Page in 1956. Strolling between its adjoining fountains is akin to perusing a huge multicultural plant emporium, with exhibits from every continent: pink-purple geraniums from Madeira and tropical trees from Africa are juxtaposed with yucca from the Americas and a gingko tree from China. In a conservatory with a gently gabled roof, giant Victoria water lilies floating in front of a dramatic anthropomorphic fountain transport you briefly to the watery jungles of the Amazon.

The Hills, which date from the 1980s, are arguably even more impressive. Steps and sloping walkways link terraces that are adorned with architectural features and surrounded by eccentric sculptures of sphinxes and crocodiles.

Music and light

Rays of light slant through the roof of the Temple of the Sun – an imposing stone building at the top of a flight of steps – illuminating agaves, aloes, and wall reliefs depicting scenes from Greek mythology. Wind chimes strike a gentle melody in the Oriental Garden, a quiet haven filled with Japanese maple, lotus flowers and rhododendrons. As one might expect in a garden once owned by a composer, there's a Greek theatre where summer concerts take place against a backdrop of sea views and exuberant foliage. Strident symphonies serenade the harmonious collection of plants.

Find Your Joy

Getting there
Ischia is easily reached by regular hydrofoils and ferries from the city of Naples. Once on the island, catch bus CS or CD, both of which stop close to the entrance to the gardens.

Accessibility
The gardens are accessible to visitors with disabilities. There are two accessible toilets and an alternative entrance at the upper level. Entrance to the garden and its concerts is free for visitors with a disability card.

When to go
Summer (June to August) is the best time for exotic plants, flowering trees, and water lilies, but the weather can be very hot. Spring (March to May) is cooler and there are flowers everywhere.

Further information
• Admission charge.
• Open April to October.
• No dogs allowed, except service dogs.
• There's a teahouse serving drinks and light snacks.
• www.lamortella.org

Other Gardens on Ischia

Giardini Ravino

Conceived by local botanist Giuseppe D'Ambra in 2006, this small garden just south of Forio is a shrine to the cactus. It exhibits a diverse collection of the prickly plants, as well as other succulent species, many of which are said to have homeopathic qualities. Alfresco art and sculpture melds cleverly with the greenery.

Don't miss

The regular music concerts

Parco Idrotermale del Negombo

Ischia's alkaline springs have been mined since ancient times. The Negombo park began to evolve in the late 1940s on the opposite side of the Zaro promontory to La Mortella, mixing imported plants with local species. Thermal pools were subsequently added, and various pieces of contemporary sculpture were introduced to complement the greenery. It is now listed as an 'art park' by the Giardini Grande Italiani.

Don't miss

Taking a dip in the thermal pools

Find artistic inspiration in a painter's garden

FRANCE

 Reflection, colour, design

 May to July

Just as when looking at one of his paintings, it's easy to lose yourself and all track of time when standing in Monet's sublime garden at Giverny. Gazing across the Water Garden pond, covered with the horizontal patterns of water lilies and the vertical reflections of willow trees, is an image that will stay with any garden lover and art aficionado forever. It's like you've stepped into one of the great artist's works.

A labour of love

The garden wasn't always as soul-stirring as it is today, though. When Monet moved here in 1883 with his two children (from his late wife) plus his mistress and her six children, they found themselves in a fruit-press

house with an orchard and kitchen garden outside. Monet immediately set to work transforming the exterior, replacing most of the trees in the orchard with metal frames for climbing roses to grasp, thus creating the Clos Normand (enclosed Norman garden). He then bought a plot of land on the other side of the railway line and crafted the Water Garden, a space that was to be a constant source of inspiration for him until his death in 1926 and a constant delight for visitors today.

Manicured wildness and Japanese influences

The skill in the Clos Normand is that while the layout was carefully planned, once the flowers were planted Monet allowed them

Right: The Water Garden: an ornamental mirror and muse for so many beloved artworks

Below: Monet's house, both inside and out, reflects the colours he loved to paint with

© NINIFERRARI / SHUTTERSTOCK

© MAISON ET JARDINS DE CLAUDE MONET - GIVERNY

Q&A

What's the best thing about working in Monet's Garden?
Planting is undoubtedly one of the best things to do, but not the easiest! Gardeners need knowledge and skills to position even the simplest flower.

How much is maintaining the garden influenced by Monet's original designs?
This is a historical garden, created from 1883 onwards, so we try to find flowers from Monet's time.

Is there a less-known section a visitor should see?
Due to the garden's popularity and small size, visitors follow well-defined paths. If some areas are off-limits, the resulting bit of mystery sparks one's imagination.

What are the challenges?
Welcoming the public while keeping on working. Each flowerbed must be planted as beautifully and quickly as possible, and remain blooming throughout the season.

What's your favourite flower or plant here?
A gardener likes all flowers and plants.

Rémi Lecoutre, Deputy Head Gardener

to run riot, creating a natural, wild effect. Along with the metal frames draped with climbing roses and clematises, height here comes from the Japanese cherry, apple and apricot trees, while the gravel paths at ground level are bordered by beds filled with jostling tulips, irises, oriental poppies, daffodils and peonies, and overrun by nasturtiums. On a warm day, as bees buzz and the flowers sway, this section of garden is enough to make anybody pick up a paintbrush.

Heading under the tunnel that connects to the Water Garden is a suitably fairy-tale-like way to arrive at this fabled location. Here, Monet's love of Japanese art and design is evident (as it is in his collection of prints in the house) in a space that was to be his muse for decades. The pond he had dug, the water lilies that carpet its surface and the Japanese-style bridge that crosses it evoke sighs and smiles. The beauty and Asian influence continue with

Opposite: The gardens of the Museo Sorolla mask the city sounds outside

Right: Monet crafted his garden into a living painting with bold blocks of colour

© IRAKITE / SHUTTERSTOCK

the bamboo, rhododendrons and Ginkgo bilobas surrounding the garden's aquatic focus, as well as the weeping willow that so elegantly drapes over the water. Imagine the artist here, out on his boat, observing the constantly changing patterns of reflected clouds, light and plants before permanently fixing them on canvas back in his studio.

Monet once said 'Apart from painting and gardening, I'm not good at anything.' Who needs more, though, when the end results are as wonderful as this garden and the art they inspired?

Don't Miss

➜ Contemplating the reflections in the Water Garden's pond

➜ Exploring the house where Monet lived and worked

➜ Pausing under the Clos Normand's climbing roses

Find Your Joy

Getting there
Vernon is the nearest train station from where, in season, a shuttle bus connects with the garden. Walking or renting a bike outside the station is another option for the 4-mile (6.5km) journey, partly following the River Seine.

Accessibility
The paths are suitable for wheelchair users and an accessible route connects the Clos Normand with the Water Garden, avoiding the tunnel.

When to go
If you've come to see the water lilies then book for late June and July. April and May are perfect for spring flowers, such as the poppies and irises Monet often depicted in his work. September and October see the Water Garden's trees at their autumnal best.

Further information
• Admission charge. Booking advised.
• Open April to October.
• No dogs allowed.
• Les Nymphéas (The Water Lilies) restaurant serves recipes Monet himself cooked.
• https://fondation-monet.com

Other Artists' Gardens

Museo Frida Kahlo, Mexico

Mexico City is home to the Casa Azul (Blue House), where Frida Kahlo was born and died. The house provides an absorbing look at Mexico's best-known painter. Outside, a courtyard garden with colourful indigenous plants and pre-Hispanic sculptures offered a refuge, an inspiration for her work – and a source for her floral accessories.

Don't miss

Seeking out Kahlo's traditional dress collection

Museo Sorolla, Spain

Spanish painter Joaquín Sorolla created three gardens around his home in Madrid. Two take their inspiration from Andalucían gardens, specifically Seville's Alcázar and Granada's Generalife; the third has a large pond, sculptures and a pergola to brighten a shaded area. All share the awareness of light that he so perfectly captured in his works.

Don't miss

The impressive collection of paintings inside the museum

© SAIKO3P / SHUTTERSTOCK

Absorb the atmosphere and aromas of Andalucía

SPAIN

♡ Serenity, fountains, mudéjar architecture

🕐 March

Walking through the gardens of Seville's 1000-year-old Christian-Moorish royal palace complex could rank as one of Spain's most majestic strolls. Shielded from central Seville by tall, crenelated walls, the gardens feel set apart – the traffic and noise replaced by slender palms, peace and the scent of citrus, jasmine, and aromatic herbs. To step into these gardens is to find an escape from the everyday.

Like the regal buildings they complement; the lush green spaces have grown organically through the ages. Today, they fill 14 acres (6 hectares) and contain over 170 species of plant, from honeysuckle to fig trees.

Peaceful patios

The gardens' antecedents lie in the half-dozen patios adjacent to the palace buildings that date from the Islamic period (pre-1248) but were substantially altered from the 16th century.

Anchored by several fountains and cooled by a welcome mixture of water and shade, these intimate spaces invite you to rediscover the symmetrical beauty of the mudéjar style so common in 14th century Seville. The Moors nurtured the idea that ornamental gardens should reflect heaven on earth. The Christians inherited this notion and amplified it. Today, after centuries of being tended by successive designers and horticulturalists, these expansive gardens have lost none of their celestial magic.

© JOSERPIZARRO / SHUTTERSTOCK

Right: Gateways lead to palm-filled Jardín de las Damas

Below: A combination of Renaissance and Islamic design forms something sublime; citrus and fountains

© JOSERPIZARRO / SHUTTERSTOCK

© KAROL KOZLOWSKI / SHUTTERSTOCK

Q&A

What's your favourite part of the gardens?
I like the very small, almost hidden patios like the Patio de Levíes or the Patio de Romero Murube, spaces where, even on days with 6000 visitors, you can find calm.

Patios. I was expecting you to have a favourite plant.
It's impossible to speak of the Alcázar without mentioning the blossom from the bitter orange trees and the four different types of jasmine with their wonderful aromas. Also, the silk floss tree with its spectacular fuchsia that flowers in autumn.

Now we're talking. What about birds. Any impressive species in the gardens?
There are peacocks, wild ducks, parrots, and hoopoes. There are also endangered greater noctule bats, which have a wingspan of up to 1m.

Manuel Hurtado, Director of Cultural Activities

© BARONE FIRENZE / SHUTTERSTOCK

© MASSIMO SANTI / SHUTTERSTOCK

Right: An 11th-century fountain burbles in the Alhambra's Patio de los Liones

Left: The Patio de las Doncellas features sunken gardens and a reflecting pool

original vegetable gardens have vanished, over 1000 orange trees remain, including one purported to be 600 years old.

Behind the Damas garden is a tiled pavilion built in the 16th century to honour the marriage of Charles V to Isabella of Portugal. On its south side, you can unravel the secrets of an intricate maze or roam the wilder Jardín Inglés, with its sturdy oaks and strutting peacocks.

Poet's corner
The more formal Jardín del Retiro was designed in the early 20th century with a discernible French influence. It's rimmed by the hedges and Alhambra-esque ponds of the Jardín de las Poetas. Here you can sit in quiet contemplation and consider the words of the Third Duke of Rivas, a poet and Seville enthusiast who wrote: 'Magnificent is the Alcázar, for which Seville is renown'd, delicious are its gardens, with its lofty portals crown'd.'

Don't Miss

→ Walking through the maze

→ Strolling along the Galeria de Grutesco

→ Admiring the Mercury Pond next to the Jardín de la Danza

A gallery for musing
The complex's most dramatic feature is the Galeria de Grutesco, an elevated gallery embellished with porticoes fashioned in the 16th century out of an old Almohad wall.

The eye is drawn to the Jardín de las Damas laid out during the Renaissance over an erstwhile Moorish *huerta* (orchard and vegetable garden). The Moors were keen agriculturalists and botanists. To them, the garden also needed to serve a practical purpose, providing food for the palace's residents. While the

Find Your Joy

Getting there
The Alcázar is in the centre of Seville in the Santa Cruz district. Easily accessible on foot, it is close to bus, tram, and metro stations.

Accessibility
Free admission for people with disabilities. There's one accessible toilet. The gardens and palaces are mostly wheelchair accessible if you stick to the gravel and stone paths. Some of the smaller gardens aren't.

When to go
The quietest time to visit these much-loved

gardens is between November and February. The orange trees start to blossom in late February, while jasmine paints the gardens white in March and April. The colours turn to fuchsia in October with the flowering of the famous silk floss trees.

Further information
• Admission charge. To cut waiting time, it

pays to pre-purchase tickets.
• Open year-round.
• No dogs allowed, except service dogs.
• There's an onsite cafe offering light meals and refreshment.
• www.alcazarsevilla. org/en

Other Moorish Gardens in Spain

Alhambra

Granada's renowned fort-palace guards one of the most famous garden complexes in Europe and remains the yardstick by which all others are measured. The courtyards and patios in the emblematic Palacios Nazaríes date from the 14th century and were conceived by the Moors as a worldly depiction of paradise. Today, these expertly tended green spaces have lost none of their heavenly appeal.

Don't miss

The fountains of the Generalife

Córdoba's Alcázar

Located beside the Guadalquivir River in Córdoba, the Alcázar de los Reyes Cristianos was once one of the main residences of Spain's Catholic monarchs, Ferdinand and Isabella. Like Seville's Alcázar, the building's 3-leveled gardens are of mudéjar origin but were remodelled in the 1950s. They are notable for their rectangular pools, grand royal statues, and neatly trimmed cypress trees.

Don't miss

The statue of the 3rd Duke of Rivas

Traverse the world's temperate zones without leaving Wales

♡ Architecture, walks, awe

🕐 April

WALES

Sometimes the whole of Carmarthenshire can feel like a giant park, with its rolling green hills, picturesque clumps of woodland and artfully ruined castles. What it most certainly doesn't have, however, is a Mediterranean climate. That's where the extraordinary Norman Foster–designed Great Glasshouse that's the centrepiece of the National Botanic Garden comes into play.

Heart of glass

There's something science fictional about this gigantic glass dome emerging out of the ground. Comprised of 785 panes, it's the largest single-span glasshouse in the world. Step inside and you're instantly transported to distant, far warmer, climes.

Paths meander through zones devoted to endangered plants from places across the planet that are deemed to have a Mediterranean climate. On a grey day, wandering among the blue flowers of the Californian lilac, the colourful cones of proteas and the firework spikes of echiums is an absolute indulgence, warming body and soul.

Beyond the temperate

As huge as it is, the Glasshouse takes up less than an acre of this 400-acre (162-hectare) site and there's lots more to explore. Take a wander through the hay meadows of the Waun Las Nature Reserve, keeping an eye out for native wildlife. This land was all once part of a country estate, which in the Regency period was transformed into an enormous landscape garden.

© DARREN BOXER

Right: The garden is a haven for threatened species including trees endemic to southern Wales

Below: The Mediterranean regions harbour 20% of the world's flowering species; a puya

Q&A

What will 'wow' us?
The majestic Great Glasshouse never fails to take your breath away. The cavernous sweep of roof and all the Mediterranean-climate-zone plants from around the world. The smell of holidays. A real show stopper.

The smell of holidays, now there's a perfume. Any favourite plants?
In the Great Glasshouse – in the Chile section – there is a strange, prickly, triffid of a flower spike that thrusts up from the ground like a giant asparagus spear and then, ever so slowly, reveals its astonishing jade-green petals with bright orange anthers – the *Puya beteroniana*. You know when it's in flower as the birds wear punky orange hairdos, stained by the pollen.

What else should we look out for?
We have a family of otters here. I've been here since 2006 and have never seen them – but plenty have.

David Hardy, Head of Marketing and Communications

The then-fashionable shift from formal gardening to landscape gardening emphasised the creation of an idealised pastoral scene, complete with water features and strategically placed groves of trees. Since 2000, substantial work has been done to restore the lakes, ponds, and paths to their glory days.

Another Regency feature to have been restored is the vast Double Walled Garden. Its stone outer walls and brick inner walls create a set of differing microclimates, designed to extend the growing periods for crops. A quarter of it is still devoted to a kitchen garden but the rest has been laid out to trace the evolution of flowering plants, based on the latest science, from water lilies to the latest cultivars.

Birds and bees
For added thrills, time your visit for one of the flying displays at the British Bird of Prey Centre. Watching captive-bred native raptors – such as hawks, falcons, kites, buzzards and eagles – swoop and soar is an awe-inspiring experience.

Other features to discover include a bee garden, an Apothecary's garden and recreated Edwardian pharmacy, a display of native Welsh plants, and a nature-themed art gallery.

You can easily spend a day here, which amply justifies the journey to what some might consider to be the middle of nowhere. But for nature lovers, escaping into the green heart of Wales is a big part of the appeal.

Opposite: White Park cattle enjoying the meadow at Dinefwr

Right: The Wallace Garden focuses on cultivated plants such as dahlias and sweet peas

© CERI BREEZE / SHUTTERSTOCK

Don't Miss

➡ **Wandering the world within the Great Glasshouse**

➡ **Finding calm on a tranquil lakeside walk**

➡ **Watching eagles dare to fly at the daily raptor display**

Find Your Joy

Getting there
The nearest train station is Carmarthen, 8 miles (13km) away. Buses are limited to the daily 279 service, which picks up at the train station mid morning and drops back later in the afternoon (check current schedule).

Accessibility
Wheelchair accessibility is excellent. All paths are wheelchair friendly. Wheelchairs (free) and mobility scooters (for hire) are available (book ahead). A shuttle buggy can take you to far-flung parts of the garden. There's also a fully accessible Changing Places toilet facility near the gatehouse.

When to go
March, April and May see bluebells and daffodils sprouting in the Springwoods, the Great Glasshouse erupting in Mediterranean colour, and birds and insects.

Further information
• Admission charge.
• Open year-round.
• Dogs on non-extendable leads are allowed on designated 'Doggy Days' (usually Mondays, Fridays and the first weekend of the month).
• https://botanic garden.wales

Other Nearby Welsh Gardens

Aberglasney

Like wandering through a scene from *Bridgerton* but with much less nudity, this exquisite garden is only a 15-minute drive from the National Botanic Garden. It was founded in Elizabethan times and its gorgeous cloister garden is the only one like it to have survived from that era. There are also two other walled gardens along with meadows and woods to explore.

Don't miss

Strolling through the 250-year-old yew tunnel

Dinefwr

Dinefwr is a large estate with a ruined 12th-century castle and a 17th-century manor house, now owned by the National Trust. You can wander here for hours, exploring the bucolic wildflower meadows, the deer park and the boardwalk through the bog woods. One path was designed by legendary landscape gardener Lancelot 'Capability' Brown.

Don't miss

The rare White Park cattle, an old breed once common in Britain

Rediscover love among Renaissance blooms

♡ Romance, history, château life

🕐 April and May

Yew trees sculpted like musical notes. Trimmed boxwoods resembling evergreen harps and lyres. A water garden where the pool of the *miroir d'eau* (water mirror) creates a bewitching kaleidoscope of light and mood. Nowhere else in France's château-strewn Loire Valley does a garden represent the wealth and taste of the French aristocracy during the Renaissance with such horticultural panache.

Completed in 1536, Château de Villandry was the last great pleasure palace to be built on the banks of the Loire. Just as the castle is filled with a succession of splendid *salons* (rooms), so is its sweep of ornamental gardens, born from the Renaissance notion that a garden is the extension of a noble interior.

Jardin à la française

Villandry was simply a medieval tower sandwiched between a forest and the same-name village when Jean Breton, the King's finance minister, acquired the estate in 1532. Having overseen the construction of nearby Château de Chambord for François I, Breton knew a thing or two about Renaissance architecture and masterpiece gardens. Strolling around Villandry today is a magnificent waltz through 17 acres (7 hectares) of French formal gardens (*jardins a la français*), covering four terraces, all meticulously recreated from 1908 onwards to look how they appeared in the 16th century.

Amour in the Love Garden

In line with Renaissance design, the ornamental gardens sit snug

Right: Box hedge hearts and daggers and topiary yews come together in the Love Garden

Below: There are a staggering 52 miles (84km) of hedging at Villandry; colour by cabbages

© RICHARD SEMIK / SHUTTERSTOCK

Q&A

Villandry's most surprising aspect?
The garden's immensity and multiple faces it is composed of. Every aspect of *l'art des jardins* (garden art) is here in one place: geometry; perspective; seasonal decorations of fruits and vegetables.

Your favourite spot in the garden?
The small wood above the last terrace. Here you find a view similar to that of a drone. This is the highest point in the garden from where you can appreciate just how much the village of Villandry is a component of the overall creation.

The most unexpected flower to track down?
I have a preference for the multi-coloured cabbages whose foliage makes a rainbow decoration in summer and autumn. It's an effect renewed every year, for more than 20 years if I remember correctly.

Georges Lévêque, author and photographer of more than 50 books on gardens

Right: Every June the Villa Ephrussi de Rothschild opens to artists for a day

Left: There's magic in the night during Les Nuits des Mille Feux

Don't Miss

→ Figuring your way out of the maze

→ Playing old-fashioned games beneath apple trees in the Chambre des Enfants (Kids' Room)

→ Visiting during Les Nuits des Mille Feux (Jul & Aug) for candle-lit walks and fireworks

against the reception halls of the château's south wing, presenting wonderful floral views for guests. The Jardin d'Amour (Love Garden) elevates nature to the highest point of perfection (with the help of 10 full-time gardeners) and is loaded with symbolism. Even die-hard cynics risk a quickening of the pulse when strolling around geometric flowerbeds whose pink, white and blood-red springtime tulips, summer begonias and dazzling mix of chiselled boxwoods portray tender, passionate, flighty and tragic love. April's glorious abundance of forget-me-nots evokes the gallant knight who died gathering these flowers for his lover, crying 'Forget me not!' The formal appearance of the garden means that you might feel somewhat under-dressed.

Awakening every sense

Turn your back on boxwood hearts and head next to the decorative potager where spring and summer planting lists read like an A to Z of a Michelin-starred kitchen garden. Arranged in nine squares, more than 20,000 red and green lettuces, purple and black cabbages and other vegetables form a dazzling chessboard of colour and form. Aromatic herbs and medicinal plants set every sense on fire in the medieval Jardin des Simples (Garden of Medicinal Plants). Or go old school with a romantic swoon over a celestial mirage of perfumed perennials blazing every colour under the sun in the Jardin du Soleil (Sun Garden).

Find Your Joy

Getting there
From nearest big town Tours, Château de Villandry is 10 miles (16km) southwest by car, or a scenic 12.5-mile (20km) bike ride; check www.loireavelo.fr for the best route. Savonnières, 3 miles (5km) northeast, is the closest train station.

Accessibility
Four parking spaces close to the entrance are reserved for visitors with disabilities. Before arriving, download a garden map showing a wheelchair-friendly itinerary. Visitor guides in Braille are available on site.

When to go
The flowers are at their blooming best April to October. Forget-me-nots and fruit trees peak in April, tulips in April and May, narcissi March to June, and begonias and yellow daisy-like bidens from July to September.

Further information
• Admission charge. Booking essential for Les Nuits des Mille Feux.
• Open year-round.
• Dogs welcome on a lead.
• Restaurant La Doulce Terrasse and sandwich kiosk open April to November.
• www.chateau villandry.fr

Other *Jardins à la Française* in France

Villa Ephrussi de Rothschild
Designed in 1905–1912 to resemble the deck of a ship when viewed from the adjoining villa, this *jardin à la française* on the French Riviera takes garden aficionados through nine themed gardens – French, Spanish, Florentine, Japanese and so on – once tended by 30 gardeners dressed as sailors wearing red pompom berets.

Don't miss
Smelling the lavender in early summer in the Jardin Provençal

Manoir d'Eyrignac
A short drive northeast of Sarlat-la-Canéda brings you to these exquisite gardens housing some of France's finest topiary art. The hornbeam, boxwood et al have been clipped meticulously by hand to create a razor-sharp menagerie of shapes and animal sculptures (cockerels, dogs, ducks, all sorts) across seven themed gardens.

Don't miss
Drinking and dancing under fireworks during a Pique-Nique Blanc (Jul & Aug). Wear white

Expand your mind at Crawick Multiverse

♡ Land art, stone circles, cosmic comprehension

🕐 June or December

SCOTLAND

I n deepest, darkest December, witnessing the arrival of the Northern Hemisphere's longest night of the year at Crawick Multiverse is magical. Stand atop the Milky Way, a spiral-form mound of earth representing our galaxy, and the sun traces the garden's North-South Path with astonishing accuracy, before sliding out of sight.

Masterminded by the American landscape designer and cultural theorist Charles Jencks, the Crawick Multiverse, in Scotland's southwestern region of Dumfries and Galloway, explores the ideas of astronomy, cosmology and space by laying out our current understanding of physics, the universe and all the possibilities beyond in human-made landforms, coiling walkways and large standing stones. It's a mind-bending experience.

It took Jencks 10 years to turn this former coal mine into a horticultural cosmos, and today, wandering through his creation is a wondrous experience. The more of the landscape that gets revealed, the more you appreciate your own minuscule standing in the universe.

Path of enlightenment

Enter via the North-South Path. Aligned with the true points of the compass, this gravel walkway is edged with huge standing stones (found on the site) and leads visitors over the crest of a hill before spilling out into our known universe.

The curved Amphitheatre ahead represents the sun – the real burning ball of hydrogen and helium drops directly down onto the path during the solstices. Lying off to the right are the Galactic

Right: Boulders atop Andromeda and The Milky Way represent cosmic phenomena

Below: The Amphitheatre faces due south and can hold 5000 people; the Multiverse

Q&A

Who was Charles Jencks?

Charles was an American academic and architect. Design was at the heart of his interests, but so were playful intellectual ideas.

Such as the multiverse. So what is it?

The multiverse concept is the idea that our universe is not the only one. If we are part of one universe, then there could be an infinite number of universes in existence that are separate from us – a multiverse.

How is this translated into garden design?

By the site being more of an art landscape using landforms and stones to represent the concepts of the multiverse. There has been planting, but it's very specific to fit with the landforms. The site was formerly an open-cast coal mine, so it's been an extraordinary feat of intellect and vision to turn it into what you see today.

Gillian Khosla, Chair of the Crawick Multiverse Trust

© CRAWICK MULTIVERSE

Collisions, a collection of rough standing stones and an arc of evergreen trees, symbolising the cymbal-crash of galaxies that birthed a billion new stars. To the path's left are Andromeda and the Milky Way, two rounded hills with snail-shell-like tracks leading to whorls of more standing stones on top, echoing the spiral shapes of the star systems that are travelling towards each other, destined to meet in four billion years' time.

The ultimate understanding
So far, so school-level science. But then Crawick drags you into its vortex because past the Milky Way is the Supercluster, a series of triangular tufts with gravel pathways that represent gravity. Their south-west layout makes their shadows dance as the sun moves. Superclusters force galaxies to line up as they do and are some of the largest known things in the universe.

Next is the Multiverse, a corkscrew of large curling stones

Opposite: In Northumberland lies the largest land sculpture in female form in the world

Right: Over 300 megalith-like boulders line the North-South Path

that were also found on site and reused. This is where the brain begins to melt as the theory that we and our universe are part of a multiverse is represented.

Nothing underscores this theory like walking to the Belvedere at the very top of the site. From here, a 360-degree view stretches out across the entire Crawick Multiverse and on to the surrounding patchwork quilt of bucolic countryside. It also plants a seed of thought that visitors will take away with them – if our universe is part a multiverse, what lies beyond that?

Don't Miss

→ Pondering the limits of cosmic knowledge from the Belvedere

→ Recharging in the Amphitheatre during the summer solstice

→ Exploring the Supercluster shadow patterns

Find Your Joy

Getting there
The nearest train station is Sanquhar, around a mile (1.6km) from the garden. No buses go from the station and taxis

should be prebooked. It's possible to walk.

Accessibility
Not all the pathways are navigable for those with mobility issues. However, wheelchair users are able to access the part of the garden known as The Desert via a separate private road. Call ahead for details.

When to go
Plan a visit for the Northern Hemisphere's summer and winter solstices (in June and December respectively) and you can experience the joy of watching the sun align with the standing stones on the longest and shortest days of the year.

Further information
• Admission charge.
• Open year-round.
• Dogs welcome.
• No cafe but small coffee machine available.
• www.crawick multiverse.co.uk

Other Land Art Gardens

Northumberlandia, England

Another Jencks creation, this huge community park took more than 1.5 million tonnes of earth, rock and clay from the former Shotton Surface Mine and reshaped them into a giant sculpture of a woman. The land form is a quarter of a mile long with paths that curl across the green hillocks that create her eyes, nose, mouth and breasts.

Don't miss
Finding the viewpoint on the woman's forehead

City, USA

Michael Heizer's grand landscaping project *City* is one of the largest artworks in the world and took 50 years to build. Heizer used materials found in the surrounding Nevada desert, including sand and huge rocks that were turned into a mega, 1.5-mile long (2.4km) abstract reinterpretation of the surroundings.

Don't miss
Admiring Complex One, inspired by Egypt's Step Pyramid of Djoser

Get drenched by 400-year-old trick fountains

♡ Thrills, architecture, opulence

◷ April and May

AUSTRIA

The reflection of a dreamy pastel-yellow palace shimmers on the still surface of an ornamental pond. A promenade leads to a Roman amphitheatre of pink mosaics and classical statues spouting water. So far, so tranquil. The guide graciously invites you to take a seat on one of the stools surrounding a grand stone table, before beginning the next segment of his talk. Who can refuse? And then ... whoosh! Suddenly water erupts all around you, including from some very unexpected places. A shriek, a jump, but it's too late – you're soaked, but grinning from ear to ear. This is the rather rude introduction to Hellbrunn Palace Gardens and its collection of trick fountains.

Naughty Prince-Archbishop
This late-Renaissance amusement park was the brainchild of the mischievous ruler of Salzburg, the Prince-Archbishop Markus Sittikus. Enchanted by what he had seen in Italian gardens, in 1612 he personally oversaw the creation of these fantasy fountains, still unique in the world today.

Walking through the ornate flower gardens of roses, lavender, busy lizzies and pansies, bubbling fountains can be found throughout. But at five specific locations visitors are enticed into rocky grottoes filled with marble statues, gilded stucco, frescoes and mosaics. Here, guides are discreetly placed to bring hidden jets into action using the original 400-year-old system of water flowing down from nearby hills.

Right: Beware the god of freshwater and the sea. Neptune takes aim in his grotto

Below: One seat at the stone table always remains dry; a more tranquil view of Hellbrunn Palace

© SULZER / HELLBRUNN PALACE

© IRISPHOTO / SHUTTERSTOCK

What does your job entail?
I basically operate the levers in the grottoes that make the trick fountains perform.

What response are you hoping for from visitors?
I'm aiming for a reaction, a surprise, and not just to get them wet. Certainly not to scare them.

Have you got a favourite trick fountain?
Definitely the Crown Grotto, where at the end I need to persuade the visitors that they will not get wet if they walk through an arch of water jets. I won't say what happens.

What about the flowers and plants in the gardens?
It's a surprisingly untamed garden. Wild garlic seems to grow everywhere in spring, and I love when the dahlias bloom in late summer.

Bryan Crawford, Hellbrunn guide

© GIMAS / SHUTTERSTOCK

© GIMAS / SHUTTERSTOCK

Right: Six vineyard terraces bathe in the evening sun at Sanssouci

Left: There are 60 acres (24 hectares) of park to enjoy including a waterpark

Don't Miss

→ Sticking your tongue out like the Germaul fountain statue

→ Walking up Hellbrunn Hill for a photogenic panorama of Salzburg

→ Soaking up the romance of the famous gazebo from *The Sound of Music* movie

In the Neptune Grotto jets unexpectedly shoot out of the floor and innocent-looking statues suddenly spray a curious onlooker. The Crown Grotto boasts a water arch cascading out of the walls. Elsewhere, moving automatons depict scenes from Greek and Roman mythology.

Fright and fun

In each of the trick fountain grottoes visitors of all ages can't help but erupt into either fits of laughter or shrieks of fright. Which was just what Markus Sittikus intended, because these highly innovative gardens were not just to amuse but also to slightly terrify guests by demonstrating his immense wealth and power. And, of course, each grotto has one dry seat reserved for the Prince-Archbishop himself.

Walking through the Bird Call Grotto, who could imagine the chirruping and tweeting come not from a recording but from water pipes, while, somehow, tortoises playfully squirt water into each other's mouths in the Venus Grotto. Finally there is the astonishing Mechanical Theatre where 142 water-powered marionettes twirl back and forth.

Pleasure palace park

The trick fountains are just a small part of Hellbrunn's sprawling estate that also includes English and French-style gardens, parkland for picnics and sport, quiet corners for meditation, and a stone theatre where concerts have been performed since 1617.

Find Your Joy

Getting there

Bus 25 takes 25 minutes from the centre of Salzburg, or 30 minutes from the train station. Alight at the 'Rathaus' stop. Or you can rent a bike and cycle the picturesque 4.5-mile (7km) route

Accessibility

The trick fountains and the palace gardens are fully accessible for wheelchair users, while the palace is not.. Wheelchairs are also available to rent.

When to go

The palace's gardens are open all year (and very pretty under a coating of snow), but the trick water fountains can't function in winter (November to February).

Further information

• Free admission to palace gardens; admission charge to trick fountains.
• Trick fountains open April to October.
• Dogs are welcome on a lead (a muzzle must be worn in the trick fountains).
• A cafe serves hot drinks and traditional pastries.
• www.hellbrunn.at

Other Palatial Fountain Gardens

Palace of Versailles, France

Landscape designer André Le Notre created the gardens for Louis XIV's Versailles 350 years ago and they remain unsurpassed today. Every Saturday night in summer the gardens and fountains light up with Les Grandes Eaux, a breathtaking Sound and Light spectacle with the cascading water jets of the Neptune Basin performing an aquatic ballet.

Don't miss
Being wowed by the dazzling fireworks at the end of the show

Sanssouci Palace Park, Germany

The 18th-century rococo palace built for Frederick the Great was christened 'sans souci' (without a care). Inspired by Versailles but less formal, there are orchards, vineyards, a Grand Canal and the Great Fountain, which shoots water over 100ft (30.5m) into the air. Frederick never saw the fountain work – it was a century after he died that technology caught up with his ambitions.

Don't miss
Visiting the palace's striking interior and Frederick's grave

Steal away to a subtropical island retreat

IRELAND

♡ History, adventure, dreamy views

◷ May

A 'paradise' was how playwright George Bernard Shaw described Garinish Island, a little pocket of glory in a sheltered bay in west Cork heated by Gulf Stream currents. It's a jewel of a place, where classical structures frame views of heather-covered mountains sliding down into inky bays, stately trees sway in the breeze and flowers bloom in a valley so fecund it's known as the 'jungle'.

An island adventure

With white-tailed sea eagles circling overhead, seals basking on rocks and mountains cradling the views, the boat trip to Garinish is a delight in itself. It's just a mile (1.6km) off the coast from Glengarriff, but the scrawny fields and stone walls of the mainland are soon swapped for lush tropical gardens, where exotic species tower above you and ornate flourishes erupt at every turn.

From the quay, a pathway leads to the formal walled garden with its rambling roses, fruit trees and ornamental flowers, and the sunken Italian garden where a long, narrow pond draws your eye from the wisteria-clad *casita* (garden house) to the beautifully proportioned Medici house. The order and composure exude an air of utter tranquillity, especially in the quiet of the early morning, but follow the trail into the 'jungle' with its giant tree ferns and everything begins to feel more exotic.

Hop across the stepping stones in the pond and you enter the aptly named Happy

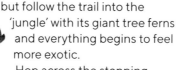

Right: Garinish combines Italianate and Arts and Crafts influences in its design

Below: The magnificent backdrop of mountain and sea; homegrown charms

Q&A

John Annan Bryce, reckless or visionary?

You have to admire his vision; he had immense foresight. Who puts their garden before their house? He had plans for a seven-storey mansion but his money was invested in Russia and he lost the lot when the Russian Revolution broke out. He had to settle for the gardener's cottage in the end.

Sounds like it's been a challenge from the start?

Oh, there's plenty of challenges. Everything has to be brought in by boat, so it takes extra time and costs more, and we're always at the mercy of the tides.

But you're still here?

Yes, it's home. I've been here 40 years, and my father worked here before me, but we're only here to preserve the garden and pass it on to the next generation.

Finbarr O'Sullivan, Horticultural Supervisor

Garinish Island

Valley, an informal glen where a tunnel of unfamiliar species forms a path from a 19th-century tower at one end to a roofless Grecian temple at the other.

Opposite: An island in the sun – Tresco Abbey's lush surrounds

Right: Seals watch the to and fro of ferries crossing to the island

Visionary creators
Once a wild and untamed islet with barely a skim of soil, Garinish (or Ilnacullin, the 'Island of Holly', as it is also known) caught the eye of Belfast-born MP John Annan Bryce and his wife Violet, a society hostess, in 1910. Its sheltered position, mild microclimate and heavy rainfall convinced them of its potential and they set about ambitious plans to transform it with the help of architect and garden designer Harold Peto. Soil and manure were brought in from the mainland, rocks blasted, and a belt of protective pine, spruce, cypress and fir trees planted along the shore, helping the island mature into a serene sanctuary for exotic species. Today bright and blousy rhododendrons and azaleas billow from the borders while palms and bamboo give structure.

An artistic retreat
In many ways the garden's legacy is one of perseverance. The Bryces' determination encouraged others, and artists and writers such as AE Russell, George Bernard Shaw and Agatha Christie loved it here. Walking Garinish's pathways, it's easy to get lost in thought, the gardens seemingly giving permission for the contemplation of grand plans and fights of fancy.

Don't Miss
→ Touring the restored rooms of Bryce House

→ Soaking up the views of the Grecian temple

→ Admiring the Italian garden's 300-year-old larix bonsai

Find Your Joy

Getting there
Access to the island is by a 15-minute boat journey from Glengarriff, County Cork. Boats run all day during the garden's open season. There is parking near the harbour and regular buses from Cork.

Accessibility
The island ferry, Bryce House, the walled garden and Italian garden are accessible for wheelchairs, but other parts of the island have steep steps or paths. There are benches to rest on and an accessible toilet.

When to go
The gardens open in April with a burst of colour from the magnolias and camellias, which is quickly followed in May by veils of vibrant rhododendrons and azaleas in Happy Valley. In June, the casita is draped in delicate wisteria and the herbaceous borders reach full glory.

Further information
• Admission charge (cash only) and ferry charged separately.
• Open April to October.
• Dogs welcome on a lead.
• Cafe on site.
• https://garinish island.ie/

Other Island Gardens

Tresco Abbey Gardens, England

A subtropical garden set around the ruins of a 12th-century Benedictine abbey, this incredible collection of 20,000 exotic species is all the more surprising, thanks to its setting on a small island 28 miles (45km) off the Cornish coast. Towering palms, cacti and flamboyant flame trees line the paths.

Don't miss
Inspecting the Valhalla figureheads and name boards salvaged from local shipwrecks

El Nabatat Island, Egypt

British army big shot Lord Kitchener indulged his love of tropical plants while transforming this small island in the Nile into a lush oasis in the 1890s. It evolved into the Aswan Botanical Gardens and a short *felucca* (wooden boat) ride takes you from city hustle to quiet lawns fringed by exotic trees, rare palms and magnificent flowers.

Don't miss
Catching the afternoon golden light and scent of sandalwood

Swoon at the romance of this quintessential English garden

♡ History, design, pleasure

🕐 June and July

ENGLAND

White, green, grey and silver: these are the only colours that writer Vita Sackville-West permitted in her White Garden at Sissinghurst. It's a bold, much copied concept for a garden, one that evokes purity while creating drama through the juxtaposition of a rich variety of shapes, textures and form. Walk the box hedge-lined paths between borders out of which grow such diverse blooms as gladioli, irises, pompom dahlias and Japanese anemones and imagine this garden as Vita did – glowing in the moonlight.

Creating a classic garden

When Vita and her husband, the diplomat and diarist Harold Nicholson, bought Sissinghurst Castle in 1930 it was a ruin in the Kent countryside with no garden to speak of. It took the couple three years to clear away the weeds and overgrowth before they could plant anything. The overall design was conceived by Harold, and the plantings by Vita, who made Sissinghurst famous through her gardening columns for the Observer newspaper.

First opened to the public in 1938, the garden and surrounding estate have been part of the National Trust since 1967. The trust's team balance respect for Vita and Harold's masterplan with necessary updates and revisions.

Vivid blocks of colour

The best way to appreciate Sissinghurst's layout is to climb to the top of the Elizabethan red brick tower at its heart – it was in here that Vita had her writing studio. From the

Right: A cacophony of pink blooming in front of the South Cottage

Below: Sissinghurst Castle in high summer; some of the 30,000 daffodils on display

© NATALIA GREESKE / SHUTTERSTOCK

© RUSANA KRASTEVA / SHUTTERSTOCK

Q&A

What makes Sissinghurst so special?
It's the setting. There's nothing dramatic here, but the garden design is so right and effortless.

How much pressure is there to keep the garden as Vita and Harold designed it?
You don't just stand still otherwise the garden would ossify. We work hard at trying to understand Vita and Harold's gardening philosophy, their likes, their dislikes. In her notebooks Vita writes 'actions'. If something wasn't working, she would try a different variety or use it elsewhere. We should be equally experimental and equally challenging ourselves.

You're lucky she recorded so much about the garden.
There's lots we don't have records for. For example, many of the daffodils in the orchard are unknown varieties – it's tricky to work out when there's 30,000 of them.

Troy Scott Smith, Head Gardener

© SUSAN WARREN PHOTOGRAPHY / SHUTTERSTOCK

© EVA NEMETH / NATIONAL TRUST

Right: The formal heart of Hever Castle gardens which sprawl over 125 acres (51 hectares)

Left: The new Mediterranean-style Delos garden

Don't Miss

→ Listening for birdsong in the Nuttery

→ Marvelling at the pleached lime trees on the Lime Walk

→ Being dazzled by dahlias in the South Cottage Garden

roof there's a grand view of the garden's mainly colour-blocked and themed 'rooms', plus more naturalistic elements such as the orchard and meadow.

Back at ground level, it's a thrilling space to explore, with openings in the clipped hedges and old brick walls providing tantalising glimpses of what lies beyond. Inhale the scent of over 200 cultivars in the Rose Garden when they are at peak bloom in late June. This very English collection of old roses and ramblers – combined with the aroma of honeysuckle – is

Sissinghurst at its most romantic. They remain as Vita once described them: pieces of beautiful embroidery in the garden's floral tapestry.

Inspired by a Greek island

One of the most engaging parts of Sissinghurst is its orchard of old Kentish fruit trees. In spring, cohorts of daffodils burst from the ground here, while in summer the meadow is filled with wildflowers.

Just when you thought Sissinghust couldn't be more English, you suddenly find yourself amid a Mediterranean landscape of cypress, fig and cork oaks sprouting from gravel with flashes of red field poppies. This is Delos, completed in 2021 but based on a 1930s project by Vita and Harold, when the couple tried but failed to recreate what they'd encountered on the namesake Greek island. They would surely be delighted at how successfully it now evokes the sun-drenched landscape of the Cyclades.

Find Your Joy

Getting there
The nearest train station is Staplehurst, about 6 miles (10km) to the north of Sissinghurst. The National Trust website has

a downloadable map of the cycling route from the station to the garden.

Accessibility
Wheelchair users and those with mobility issues will find the garden's many changes of level, steps and slopes a challenge. Pushchairs and buggies are not allowed in the formal garden. Accessible toilets are available.

When to go
Through March and April, look for muscari, dwarf irises, fritillaries, tiny rock narcissi and tulips along the Lime Walk. The Rose Garden looks good all year but is spectacular from May to August. The White Garden is at its best during July; the Cottage Garden from the end of July through August.

Further information
• Admission charge.
• Open year-round.
• Dogs welcome on a lead around the wider estate, but not in the formal and vegetable gardens.
• Cafe on site.
• www.nationaltrust.org.uk/sissinghurst-castle-garden

Other Historic Gardens in Kent

Hever Castle

Famous as the childhood home of Anne Boleyn, Hever's modern day revival dates to when William Waldorf Astor bought the property in 1903. The American tycoon supervised the creation of a splendid set of gardens including a rose garden with over 4000 bushes, a topiary chess set, a yew maze and a lake overlooked by a Japanese-style teahouse.

Don't miss
Admiring Astor's collection of classical statuary in the Italian Garden

Walmer Castle

The official residence of the Lord Warden of the Cinque Ports, this sea-facing fortress is also a delight for garden lovers. A kitchen garden was established in the 18th century and wardens down the years have added an oval lawn planted with specimen trees, a 'cloud' pruned yew-lined broadwalk and an evergreen shrubbery created in a chalk pit.

Don't miss
Wandering through the Paddock's daffodils and snowdrops in spring

Explore the impossible in a Sicilian stone quarry garden

ITALY

♡ Island adventure, geology, botany

◷ May and June

The bike ride across the butterfly-shaped island of Favignana is furnace hot and dusty. Giant blocks of tufa litter roadsides like a child's toy bricks abandoned mid-way through play. It's unfathomable that anything of beauty can grow on this sun-scorched speck in the Egadi archipelago where tuna fishers once cast their nets and *pirriaturi* cut into the land. Since Roman times these master quarrymen excavated the pale limestone to build magnificent opera houses and *palazzi* (palaces) across the water on Sicily, leaving behind open quarries and tunnels. It feels desolate – thrillingly biblical. Yet hidden in Favignana's parched interior is an extraordinary green oasis where the passion of a visionary garden-lover has achieved the impossible.

If stones could talk

Exploring labyrinthine footpaths, gravity-defying stone bridges and secret staircases in the Garden of the Impossible is a captivating journey through island geology and history. It feels like an Indiana Jones film set. Walls of golden-hued limestone embedded with shell fossils take visitors back to the last Ice Age. The Romans first exploited this calcarenite stone, but it was intensive quarrying from the 17th to 19th centuries that gave Favignana its chopped and chiselled appearance. When Palermo city native Maria Gabriella Campo married an islander and set up home on Favignana in 1967, she found herself laying out her dream garden on hostile, rocky land strewn with quarry debris. Observing traces of the

Right: A warren of shady passages reveal surprises around each corner

Below: The walls of the garden still show the stonemasons' cut marks; jacaranda in blossom

Q&A

There's a very special intimacy to Giardino dell'Impossibile. How do you explain this?
You have to think of Giardino dell'Impossibile as the beautiful dream of a lady who came from the city, a young bride who named her new home Villa Margherita after the first daises she planted around the house. It was her private garden. She never intended opening it to the public.

It looks like an archaeological site.
Yes, Maria Gabriella wanted her garden to mirror the determination and hard toil of the *pirriaturi* who worked 15 hours a day, 12 months a year to carve the landscape – her father, from Favignana, was one of those quarry stonemasons. The galleries and basins they cut are now elegant sunken Italian gardens and cool walkways, shaded from the blistering sun and protected from the salt and the wind.

Stefania Procida, Nature Guide and Garden Specialist

Giardino dell'Impossibile

© GIARDINO DELL'IMPOSSIBILE

hand tools the masons used to dig out the stone and identifying modern quarry areas where machinery was used is a trip into the garden's soul.

Marvelling at magical true tales

Standing in the shade of an old carob tree, the tour guide plucks a chocolate-brown pod dangling from a branch and snaps it open to reveal a neat row of bean-like seeds. Each is an identical weight (usually 0.2g), hence ancient Greeks using the method known to them as *keration* (carat; 'fruit of the carob') as a measure for gemstones and gold. In August when pods ripen, islanders dry the seeds to craft rosary beads or jewellery and eat the raw fleshy pods like sweets. Every native plant – there are fewer than a dozen – has a tale to tell: drought-resistant dwarf palms and prickly pears, sea buckthorn, wild rocket and laurel, aromatic fennel and thyme, asparagus and pomegranate trees.

Opposite: The beauty of Palermo's botanical gardens belie their importance as a research centre

Right: A warm and calming colour palette

Around the world in a garden

An insatiable botanist, Maria Gabriella travelled the world to source 700 different plant species – to the joy of appreciative visitors. Come here and relish the scent of roses and lavender and syrupy figs, admire delicate lotus flowers and spectacular coral trees, sway along with the tufty papyrus plants, and cool off by romantic ornamental pools adorned with moss-caked stone statues and shocking-pink water lilies. Meander slowly, revelling in the eclectic exoticism of it all.

Don't Miss

→ Smelling roses and magnolias in May and June

→ Listening to piano concerts in the sunken garden

→ Overnighting in Villa Margherita or a self-catering cottage

Find Your Joy

Getting there

Liberty Lines hydrofoils sail from Trapani on mainland Sicily to Favignana port (20-40 minutes), from where it's a 2-mile (3km) bike ride along unpaved roads. Rent wheels at the port.

Accessibility

Except for the footbridges and staircases, much of the garden is accessible for wheelchair users. Watch for tree roots and overhanging branches. Benches are scant. Bring a sunhat and plenty of water.

When to go

The garden's signature roses begin flowering in May with splendid hedgerow displays of butter yellow, double-flowered banksia roses – their perfume is heavenly. July and August raises the curtain on a profusion of fragrant white honeysuckle (*lonicera caprifolium*), traditionally believed by islanders to make dreams of marriage come true.

Further information

• Admission by guided tour only. Booking required.
• Open May to November.
• Dogs welcome on a lead.
• Cafe on site.
• www.giardinodell impossibile.it

Other Sicilian Gardens

Orto Botanico di Palermo

Discover Palermo's diverse roots mirrored in a wild cocktail of Mediterranean, tropical and subtropical flora in its botanical garden. Enter via the 18th-century gate and wander silk floss tree-shaded alleys punctuated with busts on pedestals, terracotta-potted cacti and footpaths scented with citrus fruits and fig blossom.

Don't miss

Observing birdlife and flora on the birdwatching trail

Giardino della Kolymbethra

When a break from the ruins of ancient Akragas (once the fourth-largest city in the known world) beckons, hit this lush garden. Tucked in a natural cleft between walls of soft volcanic tuff, it's a mix of olive and citrus trees interspersed with 300-plus labelled plant species.

Don't miss

Playing the adventurer in tunnels, a hypogeum and underground river on a guided garden tour

© NIKOLPETR / SHUTTERSTOCK

Be seduced by a garden of global delights

♡ Wild vegetation, seascapes, excitement

🕐 March to May

It's easy to miss the sign for the French Riviera's most original garden as the twisting road to St-Tropez veers past views of the most spectacular azure bays. But you'll know you've arrived at Domaine du Rayol as you'll get a strange sense you've walked onto the set of *The Great Gatsby* – the reception building, a palatial, pastel 1910 villa, was once home to the wealthy Courmes family who transformed it into a luxury hotel and casino, and started gardening in the grounds. As you approach, the air is filled with the aromas of the French Mediterranean: thyme, rosemary, fennel, sage, pine and other herby scents wafting up from the dense maquis that bursts with broom, daisies and violets. It all feels very chic and sensuous.

Global garden tour

Surprise and delight continue as you strike out on what is essentially a voyage around the world in gardens. First stop is the Canary Islands section with its distinctive dragon trees and rock roses, the unique flowers that bloom for just a single day. In contrast, the Chilean garden is marked by thorny puya bushes whose flowers erupt in dazzling metallic blue and fluorescent green blooms each June. And even though the plants are very different – spiky here, smooth and glossy there, both tiny and giant in scale – you'll soon notice an uncanny familiarity, that somehow they belong together. And that's no coincidence. Each garden region here has a climate that is horticulturally similar to the Mediterranean, even if it is geographically

Right: The garden trail leads to the Marine Garden, explored with a snorkel and flippers

Below: Step into the fragrant world of Mediterranean plants; a South African protea

© LENS-68 / SHUTTERSTOCK

© PACK-SHOT / SHUTTERSTOCK

Q&A

What is the best time of day for a visit?
Come for sunset on the terrace of the Hôtel de la Mer for a stunning panorama over the gardens and sea.

Which is your favourite garden?
Out of the several landscapes we have dedicated to 'guest' countries, I love the New Zealand valley where there are incredible ferns that can grow 23ft (7m) high.

And the biggest challenge tending the gardens?
This is essentially a wild garden where we respect nature as much as possible, so our small methods for maintaining some order need to be very subtle so the visitor does not really notice our work.

Tao Ramsa, Head Gardener

© GARDENS BY DESIGN / SHUTTERSTOCK

© ALAIN KUBACSI / GETTY IMAGES

Right: A sun trap for cacti and agave in the Jardin Exotique d'Èze

Left: Prickly pears and fox tail agave thrive in the Arid American Garden

Don't Miss

→ **Summer snorkelling in the Marine Garden**

→ **Hunting down the century-old great nolina**

→ **Taking an aromatic stroll through the wild maquis**

far away. The Canary Islands, Australia, California, South Africa and Chile are all represented alongside the Mediterranean itself. There are also four 'guest' gardens honouring regions with slightly drier or more tropical climes: Mexico, New Zealand, subtropical Asia and subtropical America. You'll spy the red fingers of Australia's kangaroo paw, and the huge protea flowers from South Africa. Most of the plants might not be from here, but they've asserted their claim and are flourishing, and it's energising to witness them thrive.

Walk on the wild side

Things weren't always so secure, however, as while some of the plants here are a century old, the site was nearly cleared in the 1980s when developers made plans to create a holiday resort. In 1989, France's Conservatoire du Littoral (coastal protection agency) stepped in to buy the land and ensure permanent protection, appointing renowned garden designer, Gilles Clément, to landscape the grounds into what you see today.

Clément was an ecological innovator, and one of his concepts, the *jardin en mouvement* (moving garden) was particularly fitting for this pristine natural environment: plants here are allowed to grow freely and evolve as nature intended with minimal tending. It is perhaps this ethos that helps the strikingly different gardens blend into a naturalistic whole, and become a homage to the enchantment of the Mediterranean.

Find Your Joy

Getting there
Buses 7801 and 7803 run along the coast between Toulon and St-Tropez, dropping visitors at Le Rayol tourist office, a

15-minute walk from the gardens. There is parking.

Accessibility
Six of Rayol's gardens are easily accessible, as are the cafe, bookshop, and concert and exhibition venues. The rest of the site is spread over different levels linked by staircases.

When to go
Each season offers

something different: perfumed Mediterranean spring flowers from March to May; Mexican cacti in the dry summer months of July and August; and Australian mimosas and South African protea in December and January.

Further information
• Admission charge.
• Open every day except 25 December.

• No dogs allowed.
• On-site refreshments at Le Café des Jardiniers.
• www.domaine durayol.org

218 France

Other Gardens on the French Riviera

Jardin Botanique
Val Rahmeh-Menton

In the heart of the port of Menton, this botanic garden provides an oasis of calm the moment you walk through the ornate gates and along a shady palm-lined drive. Non-native plantings include cacti, bamboos, flowering hibiscus, plus lotuses and giant water lilies. There is also a Mediterranean landscape of olive groves and citrus trees.

Don't miss
Spotting the edible plants among the collection

Jardin Exotique d'Èze

The tiny village of Èze perches high above the Mediterranean, its exotic gardens climbing up arid, rocky outcrops to the ruins of a medieval castle. The view becomes ever more spectacular as you weave past caves and cascades planted with exceptional yucca, agave and other cacti. Dotted along the path are tempting deckchairs for a spot of sunbathing/plant-spotting.

Don't miss
Relaxing by the waterfalls of the subtropical Espace Zen

Fall under the spell of potentially poisonous Alnwick Garden

♡ The maze, fountains, education

🕐 May

ENGLAND

Enter the Alnwick Garden either on the hour or half hour and your first word will be 'wow'. In front of you rises the Grand Cascade, a tiered series of waterfalls that perform every 30 minutes, marching down sandstone steps, framed by curving tunnels of hornbeam. Photos snapped and excellent first impressions made, it's time to explore the rest.

A garden with a goal
Alnwick is divided into different 'rooms', self-contained sections each with their own theme and feel, connected by winding paths. It's a garden with its roots (pun intended) in the Georgian period, so taking a turn through these 'rooms' is the perfect way to get the 'grand tour'. Head left of the Grand Cascade towards the black railings of the Poison Garden. When Jane, Duchess of Northumberland, began redeveloping the rundown site in 1996 the goal was not just to make something for garden lovers but to establish a charity to help with local social problems, including isolation, poor health and drug abuse. The Poison Garden was key to that plan, educating visitors about the dangers of drug-producing plants, and a guided tour here is eye-opening. That lovely laburnum? Lethal. As the signs on the always locked gates warn you: 'THESE PLANTS CAN KILL'.

There's a much more soothing experience in the Japanese cherry tree orchard, where you can sit on a swing under the delicate blossom of 326 Tai-haku trees, the world's biggest collection. Peak pink-petals season is

Right: The pools of the Grand Cascade are the backdrop to frequent marriage proposals

Below: Alnwick's kitchen garden in full bloom; the cherry orchard

© ALNWICK GARDEN

© ALNWICK GARDEN

Q&A

What effect has the garden had?
It's helped regenerate this part of Northeast England, creating a popular tourist attraction and local employment. Its charitable work combats loneliness and teaches kids the pleasure of gardening.

Assuming they don't break into the Poison Garden. How has the garden's affected you?
I helped develop the Roots and Shoots Garden where children grow their own food. Many don't know that carrots come out of the ground, so seeing a child produce vegetables gives me great job satisfaction.

**Chefs too, probably.
Your must-see?**
The Ornamental Garden. The extensive plant collection offers something of interest in every season. Its huge selection of herbaceous perennials is a passion of mine.

*Trevor Jones, Head Gardener/
Operations Manager*

© ALNWICK GARDEN

Alnwick Garden

© JIRI VONDROUS / SHUTTERSTOCK

in April, but swinging back and forth is relaxing at any time. Nearby is a 200-year-old sycamore, the oldest tree here, twisted over the centuries into gnarled magnificence. Just beyond, the Ornamental Garden, enclosed within high 18th-century walls, is similarly old and presents a charming mix of manicured formality and overflowing planting. One month you'll be loving the lilacs, the next you'll be delighted by the delphiniums.

Lost and found

Continuing clockwise leads down to the Rose Garden, where deciding which scent is your favourite can be time-consuming but fun. Sense of smell satisfied, test your sense of direction in the Bamboo Labyrinth's curving tunnels of whispering stems. An apt Latin inscription in the centre translates as 'Visitors, you have seen everything. We thank you. Now happily get lost'.

Opposite: The Peace Maze was the world's largest hedge maze until 2007

Right: Visitors have been known to faint inhaling the toxic fumes of the Poison Garden

The Labyrinth maze escaped, next up is the Serpent Garden, a collection of seven mesmerising water features, where you learn about the physics that powers them. Stand too close and you'll learn how cold the water is too.

Your visit doesn't end with the garden proper. Just outside is the Roots and Shoots Garden (a community programme for older people and children) and the Treehouse (one of the largest in the world) where your tour finishes with the best of Northumbrian food served in handsome wooden surroundings.

Don't Miss

→ Taking the perilous Poison Garden tour

→ Finding your way through the rustling Bamboo Labyrinth

→ Sitting on a swing under the cherry blossom

Find Your Joy

Getting there

The garden is in the centre of Alnwick, just off the A1 motorway that runs between London and Edinburgh, and 4 miles (6.4km) from Alnmouth railway station, served by trains between the two capitals (buses connect the station with Alnwick).

Accessibility

Gently sloping paths connecting its various sections make the garden very accessible; motorised scooters can be booked in advance.

When to go

April is cherry blossom season; May to August sees the Ornamental Garden in full flower (and the most visitors); autumnal colours from September to November are beautiful; a Christmas lights display brightens dark December.

Further information

• Admission charge for adults, with up to four children free.
• Open February to December.
• No dogs allowed, except assistance dogs.
• Two cafes and The Treehouse restaurant.
• www.alnwickgarden.com

Other Maze Gardens

Peace Maze, Northern Ireland

Planted by locals in 2000 with 6000 yew trees, this labyrinth has two distinct sections – reflecting the sectarian divisions that plagued the country for decades – which come together in the centre. The hedges themselves are purposely low (5ft/1.5m) to encourage dialogue between visitors.

Don't miss

Ringing the Peace Bell when you reach the maze's middle

Villa Pisani, Italy

Of the Veneto's many wonders, Villa Pisani stands out for its grand palace, formal gardens and beautiful maze. The latter, nine concentric circles of high hedges and dead ends, has baffled visitors since Venetian Doge and villa builder Alvise Pisani laid it out 300 years ago. Aim for the Minerva statue – once there, climb the spiral staircase to figure out where you went wrong.

Don't miss

Visiting the villa and gardens too

Marvel at ostentatious baroque design in Lake Maggiore

ITALY

♡ Peacocks, sculpture, surprise

🕐 April

ooking as impressive from a distance as they do close-up, the steeply terraced gardens of Isola Bella rise above the waters of Italy's Lake Maggiore like a leafy green ocean liner against a backdrop of red-roofed houses and snowcapped Alpine peaks. Even by the ostentatious standards of the Italian lakes, it's an arresting sight that makes you feel as if you've just woken up in a historical costume drama where flamboyantly dressed aristocrats stroll stately lawns.

Ethereal beauty

It's hard to imagine that less than 400 years ago, the island was little more than a rocky crag. The transformation began in 1632 when Carlo III, scion of the noble Borromeo clan,

initiated work on an ambitious garden and mansion that he named in honour of his wife Isabella. The work lasted 40 years and was finished off by his son, Vitaliano in around 1671. The result was other-worldly. Taking up three-quarters of 14-acre (6-hectare) Isola Bella, the gardens appear so imposing and larger than life that, from the water, they almost look as if they have been digitally enhanced.

While the first view of the complex is from a boat, the second is more subtle. After touring the rooms of the adjoining palazzo, visitors are deposited at the doors of a small courtyard fashioned with an elegant staircase. Follow the steps up between the tall hedges and prepare to be astonished.

© WESTEND61 / GETTY IMAGES

Right: Seventeenth-century statues, populate the Teatro Massimo

Below: The astonishing Isola Bella seems to glide through the water; a noble resident

© SAIKO3P / SHUTTERSTOCK

Q&A

Tough surroundings for a gardener. What's the busiest time of year?
Spring, when gardeners work in preparation for the opening season; and autumn, at the end of the season, when they must move plants and install greenhouses.

If you had to pick just one thing, what's your favourite feature?
The Rose Terrace that blooms in May. We have two special varieties: blaze, with its cherry red colour, and claire matin with its peach pink tones. The corollas of the blaze rose can be round or cupped and generally grow in small bunches composed of three to ten flowers; the claire matin has buds with a coral pink tone that first become salmon pink when they open and finally peach pink.

For the white peacock fans, how many are there?
Ten peacocks (five male, five female), and around 80 lovebirds.

Mario Mirani, Head of Garden

© SINA ETTMER PHOTOGRAPHY / SHUTTERSTOCK

© ELESI / SHUTTERSTOCK

Right: The imposing Isola del Garda is only 230ft (70m) wide

Left: In true baroque style, the gardens epitomise man's mastery over nature

Don't Miss

→ Watching white peacocks unfurl their feathers

→ Admiring the stout but noble 200-year-old camphor tree

→ Touring the rooms of the adjacent Palazzo Borromeo

Theatre of dreams

The centrepiece of the luxuriant greenery is the impossible-to-miss Teatro Massimo, which looks more like a church than a garden from ground level. This ornate baroque edifice upon which the garden's 10 exuberant terraces are stacked is punctuated with grotto-like arches and mythological statues. The vast pyramidal structure is topped by a heraldic image of a unicorn (the symbol of the Borromeo family) and linked by a series of stairways and gravel paths flanked by climbing greenery. The unashamed extravagance buoys your mood and lightens your spirit. It's impossible not to admire the unbridled ambition of the architects who built this.

Drenched in colour

While the overall impression screams baroque, the gardens retain a veneer of classical symmetry with well-trimmed lawns edged by low-cut hedges and strategically placed plant pots. The flowers are profuse, some planted in beds, others in pots or climbing up the terraced walls. It's possible to enjoy lilac wisteria in April, red and pink roses in May, and fuchsia azaleas in June. The resident white peacocks strut around whatever the season.

With roots in the 17th century, some of the gardens' plants are as old as the palazzo. There's a European yew thought to have been planted in 1700, a cork oak dating from around 1800 and a camphor tree from the 1820s.

Find Your Joy

Getting there

Ferries run approximately every half hour to Isola Bella from the lakeside towns of Stresa and Verbania Pallanza.

Stresa is an hour by train from Milan.

Accessibility

The terraces may prove difficult for individuals with mobility issues. People with disabilities are entitled to a 50% ticket discount. The Palazzo is equipped with a lift and the exit turnstiles may be opened on request to aid smoother access.

When to go

The shoulder months of May and September are less crowded. May, although potentially rainy, is when the garden exhibits its best blooms, especially roses. The Palazzo and gardens are closed in the winter.

Further information

• Admission charge. Booking not mandatory, but recommended.
• Open mid-March to end of October.
• No dogs allowed, except service dogs.
• The complex has a cafe serving drinks, sandwiches, cakes, and cheeseboards.
• www.isoleborromee. it/en/isola-bella

Other Gardens in the Italian Lakes

Isola Madre

The largest of the three main Borromean islands, Isola Madre's stately gardens were designed in the English style in the early 19th century. Loved for its camellia collection, and ten different types of palm tree, the island is dominated by a huge Kashmir cypress tree dating from the 1860s which was nearly felled by a 2006 storm. Today, it's held up by cables.

Don't miss
Climbing the alfresco staircase covered with wisteria

Isola del Garda

A long, sinuous nodule of land on Lake Garda, this 17-acre (7-hectare) island is lorded over by the ornate Venetian Villa Borghese Cavazza. Formal gardens from the 19th century lie in its shadow while a less structured park extends beyond. The Italian garden has some elaborately patterned hedges, while the English garden displays an abundance of fruit trees.

Don't miss
Looking down on the lake and gardens from the main terrace

Oceania

See the beauty in an arid Australian Garden

♡ Native flora, land art, surprise

🕐 September to November

AUSTRALIA

Seeing something extraordinary that has been created from something quite the opposite is truly life-affirming. This garden in Melbourne's outer suburbia is created on a despoiled landscape by a group of botanists and local volunteers driven by a passion to regenerate native bushland. It's a remarkable accomplishment, showcasing the unique flora that thrives in Australia's diverse and hauntingly beautiful natural landscapes.

Rubbish to riches
On the land of the Boonwurrung people and surrounded by one of the few local tracts of native bushland never cleared by settlers, the Cranbourne gardens are a work in progress that began in the 1970s and opened to the public in 2006. Six walking trails and a cycling trail can be explored in the bushland, but the focal point is the site's Australian Garden. Entering, visitors are confronted with the truly breathtaking Red Sand Garden, an evocation of the arid landscape of the Red Centre. This is land art on a massive and magnificent scale, built where an ugly sand quarry and rubbish dump were previously located. Demanding admiration, it's a sight that makes the heart soar and the mind re-evaluate traditional notions of what makes a landscape beautiful. Awe-inspiring rather than picturesque, it demonstrates that beauty comes in many forms and can, like the saltbush that is planted here, flourish in even the most inhospitable conditions.

© ROYAL BOTANIC GARDENS CRANBOURNE

Right: Hop across the lily pad bridge to the Gondwana Garden's rainforest plants

Below: A true spectacle – the Red Sand Garden; paddling in the Rockpool Waterway

© JUSTIN MENEGUZZI / ROYAL BOTANIC GARDENS CRANBOURNE

Q&A

Do you have a favourite tree or plant in the garden?
Seriously! Do I have a favourite child? Different plants shine in different seasons.

So much seasonal beauty too. But what do you say to people who describe Australian native plants as ugly?
Australian plants got a bit of a bad rap during the 1950s and '60s, with the misconception that you only used Australian plants in a 'bush garden' aesthetic. Some gardens of this style looked straggly and unkempt. One of our aims is to dispel this myth and show that Australian plants are versatile, beautiful and suited for use in a huge range of garden settings and styles.

Chris Russell, Executive Director

© VITTORIO / ROYAL BOTANIC GARDENS CRANBOURNE

Royal Botanic Gardens Cranbourne

© VITTORIO / ROYAL BOTANIC GARDENS CRANBOURNE

Artful displays

After the visual wham-bam of the Red Sand Garden, the Rockpool Waterway backed by a rust-red Escarpment Wall by sculptor Greg Clark offers a bit of whimsy. Excited children hop from flagstone to flagstone in shallow waters that ebb and flow, referencing the life-giving passage of water through the Australian landscape. It's one of many playful features that landscape architects Taylor Cullity Lethlean and plant designer Paul Thompson have incorporated into the garden's design – others include a bridge resembling clumps of lily pads, a Weird and Wonderful garden with a bizarre bottle tree, and a Seaside Garden complete with abandoned flip-flops that evoke fond memories of Aussie beach holidays.

Feast for the senses

There are over 100,000 plants from 1900 plant varieties on show in the garden, over 20 of

Opposite: Peace in the city: the Royal Botanic Gardens Melbourne

Right: Wetland gardens, such as Melaleuca Spits, provide a refuge for birds at Cranbourne

which are endangered or rare and threatened species. The Ephemeral Garden in front of the visitor centre, where a riot of vibrantly coloured, drought-resistant wildflowers – such as the remarkable Big Red (*Anigozanthos*) – inevitably elicits gasps of admiration. In the Peppermint Grove, aromatic plants and trees – including Eucalyptus and Acacia – evoke the magical and calming scents of the bush. Shaded seating and deckchairs around the lake are perfect spots for quiet reflection at this special place.

Don't Miss

→ Jumping from flagstone to flagstone in the Rockpool Waterway

→ Admiring the majestic Red Sand Garden

→ Discovering different species of Australia's symbolic tree on the Eucalyptus Walk

Find Your Joy

Getting there
The gardens are 2.7 miles (4.4km) south of Cranbourne train station. Buses travel south from Station St to the

South Gippsland Hwy, stopping at Bullarto Rd, from where it's a 1.7-mile (2.8km) walk west.

Accessibility
All paths in the Australian Garden are suitable for those using electric scooters and non-motorised wheelchairs, and both are available for free hire at the visitor centre. Audio-descriptor

tours by trained staff and volunteers can be booked ahead of visits.

When to go
The garden is at its most colourful from late August to mid-January. The Acacias offer yellow sprays of colour during June, July and August; and Kangaroo Paws come into their own in September to early December.

Further information
• Free admission.
• Open daily, year-round.
• No dogs allowed, except assistance dogs.
• Cafe and kiosk on-site.
• www.rbg.vic.gov.au/cranbourne-gardens

Other Melbourne Gardens

Cruden Farm

The garden at the former home of Sir Keith and Dame Elisabeth Murdoch (Rupert's parents), was designed by landscape designer Edna Walling in the 1930s and the was largely realised by Dame Elisabeth, who oversaw plantings over eight decades. Highlights include the main driveway, planted with over 100 lemon-scented gum trees, and the bloom-filled picking garden.

Don't miss

Venturing into the secret walled garden

Royal Botanic Gardens Melbourne

Home to over 8500 species of plant from around the globe, this impressive botanical garden was established in 1846 and is one of Melbourne's greatest treasures. The 94-acre (38-hectare) site includes an interactive children's garden, an Australian forest walk, a fern gully, a cacti and succulent garden, a palm lawn, and an important collection of orchids.

Don't miss

Picnicking on one of the lawns surrounding the ornamental lake

Recharge amid nature in Aotearoa's urban ecosanctuary

♡ Birdsong, forested walks, rejuvenation

🕐 November

NEW ZEALAND

For such a visually spectacular environment, the initial thrill of entering Zealandia is actually an aural one. A chorus of bird calls erupts as you step into the world's first fully fenced urban ecosanctuary – 556 acres (225 hectares) of native forest located minutes from New Zealand's capital, Wellington.

Once past the protective gates, other senses kick in. Dappled sunlight filters down through the forest canopy, while the distinctive aroma of New Zealand bush drifts up from mosses and ferns. It's a combination of sensations that provides a re-energising escape just a short distance from the busy city.

Zealandia opened in 1999 with an ambitious 500-year vision to restore an area of forest and fresh water to its pre-human state. Until 800 years ago, New Zealand had a unique and isolated ecosystem that was almost completely mammal-free. With the arrival of Polynesian and European settlers and their mammalian pests, the country's extraordinary wildlife started to disappear. By the 1990s, Wellington was in an ecologically poor state with much native fauna and flora at risk of extinction.

Avian superstars

Since opening, Zealandia has helped reintroduce 18 species into the area, and the project is particularly credited with restoring urban birdlife to Wellington. Kākā (native New Zealand parrots, once extremely rare in the region) regularly

Right: Back from the brink – kākā parrots are now a common sight (and sound) in Wellington

Below: Zealandia's mammal-proof fence is the key to its success; freedom to thrive

© ABHISHEK R SAWANT / SHUTTERSTOCK

© ROB SUISTED / ZEALANDIA

Q&A

What's your role at Zealandia?
I'm a visitor experience volunteer guide, a photography tour guide and a Zealandia by Day guide.

Sounds busy. What are your favourite birds to photograph?
The tiny tītitipounamu (rifleman), the rare hihi (stitchbird) and the flightless takahē.

Where's best in Zealandia for visitors to take good photos?
You're virtually guaranteed a close-up experience with kākā, hihi, or korimako (bellbirds) at the feeding stations along Lake Rd.

And some special photography tips?
Get good light on the subject – from late morning onwards is best – and change the angle of the shot. Get low, almost at ground level if the bird is on the ground, and capture something that people aren't seeing with their own eyes.

Scott Langdale, Volunteer Guide and Photographer
@scottsphotosnz

© DANE GRAHAM / SHUTTERSTOCK

© PETE MONK / ZEALANDIA

Right: Threatened species prosper in Sanctuary Mountain Maungatautari

Left: The Karori Reservoir has been supplying water to Wellington since 1874

Living dinosaurs

The experience of Zealandia is often likened to *Jurassic Park*, and not just because of the fences. Tuatara, New Zealand's endemic reptiles, have changed little since they roamed Earth with dinosaurs. Spot them sunning themselves on banks along Zealandia's main trail. An insectophobe's worst nightmare, the wētā punga (a type of giant flightless cricket) grows up to 3 inches (7.5cm) long and can be seen crouched on paths during night tours. Cave wētā – watch out, they can jump up to 10ft (3m) – are also nocturnal. Skinks, geckos and frogs complete Zealandia's roll call of reptiles and amphibians.

As for the plants, the native forest is dense, tangled and evergreen. Look out for the kōtukutuku (the world's largest tree fuchsia) and the ponga (silver fern), the iconic symbol of New Zealand; by moonlight, its silvery fronds lead travellers from darkness to safety.

Don't Miss

➡ Being surprised by a kākā's stunning plumage

➡ Hearing (and hopefully seeing) a kiwi after dark

➡ Learning about natural history and Māori legends at Zealandia's visitor centre

swoop in to land on trailside feeding stations, their austere outer plumage revealing glimpses of vibrant orange when they open their wings. Scratch the forest debris with a stick and toutouwai (NZ robins) bounce in to see what's to eat. And the country's nocturnal national bird, the kiwi, is often spotted during guided night and dawn tours. Around the Karori Reservoir, the endangered takahē – only 400 of the squat swamp hens exist nationwide – patrol the waterway's grassy banks.

Find Your Joy

Getting there
Catch Zealandia's free shuttle bus from near Wellington's i-site visitor information centre. Public buses from central Wellington stop a two-minute walk from Zealandia. From the city centre it's a 3-mile (5km) drive but there's limited public parking.

Accessibility
Zealandia's main trail is well-graded and accessible for wheelchair and mobility scooter users. Other, more rugged trails in the surrounding forest are not suitable. Service dogs are only allowed based on prior approval in meeting biosecurity requirements.

When to go
Visit from October to December (spring in New Zealand) when birds are more active and vocal while breeding – you may see chicks. It's also spring flower season.

Further information
• Admission charge.
• Open daily, year-round. Booking ahead recommended for Dawn Tours, Twilight Tours and Zealandia by Night tours.
• No dogs allowed.
• Cafe on site.
• https://visitzealandia.com

Other New Zealand Ecosanctuaries

Sanctuary Mountain Maungatautari

In South Waikato's dairy farming country, this sanctuary's pest-proof fencing encircles an extinct volcanic cone, and opportunities to explore include the cross-mountain Wairere Traverse trail and tours with local Māori featuring traditional *rongoā* (Māori healing and medicine). Denizens of Maungatautari's forest include tuatara, kiwi and 20 other native bird species.

Don't miss

Joining a guided tour of the Tautari Wetlands

Orokonui Ecosanctuary

Near Port Chalmers, this predator-free nature reserve is a mainland refuge for species usually only found on New Zealand's offshore islands. Birds include the takahē and the colourful pūtakitaki (paradise shelduck), while six species of lizards and two frog species also call the sanctuary home. Book ahead for a guided tour of Orokonui's cloud forest.

Don't miss

Seeing chicks and fledgelings in November

Go bush and have a ball

♡ Escape, bush walks, unique blooms

🕐 September

AUSTRALIA

Forget any fuddy-duddy ideas about a day out in a botanic garden. The Australian Botanic Garden, southwest of Sydney, is unlike anything you could imagine. For starters, although it's in the middle of one of the fastest growing residential regions in the country, it's managed to remain an oasis of undulating green countryside and gardens. Explore, discover and enjoy and you'll feel as if you've 'gone bush' (Australian for going back to nature) and left civilisation behind. What was once old farming land, with just a patch of endangered native vegetation left, has been transformed over 40 years into a garden that showcases native plants from across Australia's vast continent.

Colourful displays, including vibrant pink, white and yellow paper daisies, greet visitors – bring a picnic to enjoy among the groves of wattle, bottlebrush or shady gum trees.

While you can tackle the Australian Garden on foot, with bushwalks from 50 yards (50m) to 12.5 miles (20km) in length including a gentle walk up Mt Annan, you can also drive a 9-mile (15km) circular route, stopping off along the way to immerse yourself in the plants that are curated by family groups and close associations. It's a botanic journey that allows you to get lost in the beauty of Australia's unique flora.

Water, water everywhere
The garden's climate is naturally hot and dry for much of the year, which makes the vast

Right: Nosing around - echidnas are one of the only surviving mammals to lay eggs

Below: The garden is famous for its springtime display of paper daisies; views from Sundial Hill

© GLENN SMITH PHOTOGRAPHY

© GLENN SMITH PHOTOGRAPHY

Q&A

Why should we visit?
To escape the busyness of the world and to discover the sheer wealth and variety of native Australian plants spread across the site.

It's a big garden, how do you see it all?
Yes, it's Australia's largest botanic garden by a long shot, but it's accessible by road. Do it on foot, on a bike, by car, or just stop at the Connections Garden, in the heart of the space, for a taster of what's on offer.

What garden experiences grab you?
In September the paper daisies are quite something. So many people wanted selfies with our flowers that we placed flat rocks to stand on to help get that special shot.

Sounds like a happy place.
Yes, I love to see people relaxing and enjoying being here – their faces say it all.

Michael Elgey, Curator Manager

© GLENN SMITH PHOTOGRAPHY

© ANNA CALVERT / GETTY IMAGES

Right: Learn about extreme conditions at the Arid Lands Botanic Garden

Left: Permanent and temporary sculptures offer stony contrast to the plants

wallabies, echidnas and koalas. Keep your eyes peeled for movement as you wander.

The 'sciencey' bit

The garden is all about living plants – there were 182,820 of them at last count, not including natural pockets of remnant bushland – but it's also home to the National Herbarium and the PlantBank, both part of the scientific side of the botanic garden. Visitors can head inside the sustainable, architect-designed Herbarium building with its soaring roof to view what happens as seed collections and plant specimens are preserved and documented. There are also historical artefacts to see, such as specimens collected by Sir Joseph Banks in 1770 when he journeyed across the oceans with explorer Captain James Cook to chart the east coast of what is now called Australia. You can even play botanist yourself when volunteers offer tours.

Don't Miss

→ Climbing Mt Annan to enjoy the views

→ Learning about Australia's diverse flora in the Connections Garden

→ Relaxing beside the lake and counting the birdlife

lake and network of creeks and temporary water courses here a welcome, cooling relief. It's also home or temporary resting place for thousands of bird species including the rare Australian swift parrot and Latham's snipe, which breaks its 12,500-mile (20,000km) migratory journey from the subarctic to spend time here. Check the garden's website for information about early morning bird walks.

It's not just flying animals you'll find though. As this is a native garden there are also resident locals including kangaroos,

Find Your Joy

Getting there
Driving is the easiest way to get here and explore what's on offer. Nearest train stations are Campbelltown and

Macarthur, from where you can catch a bus (alight at Mt Annan Drive) for a 1.2-mile (2km) walk to the entrance. The garden also has cycle trails. Bring your own bicycle or rent one in nearby Narellan.

Accessibility
The garden is accessible for wheelchairs and there are accessible toilets on site.

When to go
Discover dazzling yellow wattles blooming in June. In mid-September, it's a riot of paper daisies. A handy month-by-month flowering guide is available online to help plan a tour.

Further information
• Free admission. No booking required, but check times for guided

walks, tours and special activities.
• Open year-round.
• No dogs allowed.
• Cafe on site.
• www.australian botanicgarden.com.au

Other Native Australian Gardens

Olive Pink Botanic Garden

This space in Alice Springs is filled with native plants developed by a true eccentric, Miss Olive Pink, from the 1950s until her death in 1975. Fuel your exploration with breakfast at the cafe then stroll amid acacias, desert gums and indigenous grasses. Wear comfortable shoes and take water. This red desert land, traditional home of the Arrernte people, will captivate your heart.

Don't miss

Admiring the glowing-white trunks of the ghost gum trees

Australian Arid Lands Botanic Garden

Set above the Upper Spencer Gulf in Southern Australia's Port Augusta, this botanic garden highlights plant species that grow in the extreme conditions of Australia's arid lands, that is areas that receive less than 12 inches (30cm) of rainfall a year. Explore the fragile ecosystems of Australia's red sand planes, salt bush and desert.

Don't miss

Searching out the blood-red Sturt's desert pea

Find solace in this Sydney guerilla garden

 Whimsy, art, views

 September to November

AUSTRALIA

Sometimes an artist just needs to find their medium. So it was for Wendy Whiteley, who transformed a trash heap on a piece of unused railway land into an urban oasis. Her guerilla garden, created without a plan, on land she didn't own, and without permission, is now one of Sydney's most magical public spaces.

From sadness, beauty

Whiteley and her husband, the renowned artist Brett Whiteley, moved into a ramshackle old house in Sydney's harbourside Lavender Bay neighbourhood in the 1970s. Here they raised their daughter, Arkie, in bohemian style. One of Brett Whiteley's favourite subjects was the view of Sydney Harbour from their living room, often with Wendy's nude form in the foreground.

But Brett could never get away from his longstanding drug addiction, and he died of an overdose in 1992. In her grief, Wendy began to clear the rubbish-covered and vine-tangled plot of land by an abandoned railway adjacent to their home. She planted the steep slopes and narrow gullies with whatever took her fancy – fig trees and bangalow palm, fuchsias and golden wattle, jasmine and ferns and trumpet vines. With no horticultural training, she was guided entirely by aesthetics and instinct. A little more colour here, something a bit splashy over there. Brett had been the known artist, but now it became clear that Wendy was one too, only with plants instead of paint on her palette.

Tragedy struck again in 2001 when Arkie, Brett and Wendy's daughter, died of cancer, aged 37.

Right: Cherubs, statues, and found objects keep Wendy company

Below: The iconic view from the garden; the solo gardener is now helped by an army of volunteers

Q&A

What do visitors find most surprising about the garden?

The mere fact that the garden is there at all. Visitors are surprised to find such a haven in the city and delight in its many winding paths and quirky features with suddenly revealed views to either more pathways that demand exploration, or views of the city and harbour beyond.

How does the garden change with the seasons?

The main way it changes is down to the intensity of the sun. During a hot summer, the cool green dark of the shaded paths creates a contrast. In winter, the lower sun can reach protected areas enabling year-round enjoyment. It is mostly in shade and green but shots of crimson iresine add stabs of colour. Bromeliads in many varieties display unique flowers. Native bottlebrush and grevilleas keep the birds happy.

Ian Curdie, Volunteer Coordinator

The Joy of Exploring Gardens **243**

Right: Occasional open-air services are still held at St Dunstan in the East

Left: Wendy's garden is part of the peaceful Lavender Bay Parklands

by residents of Sydney's lower North Shore. Visitors can wander between sun and shade, admiring 'artefacts' ranging from sculptures by well-known artists to old wheelbarrows and children's toys decaying poetically between plantings. Paths zigzag through the garden, their handrails made from the limbs of fallen gum trees.

Open to the public all day, every day, the garden is a spot for intimate picnics, afternoon sunbathing or meandering walks alone with your thoughts. It's the kind of place where you can giggle with friends over a sandwich, or have a good long cry in the enveloping shade of a palm tree. On quiet mornings, your only company will be the birds – parrots and seagulls, kookaburras and brush turkeys.

Wendy's garden is a gift from one woman to an entire city, and stands as proof that a single person can change the world, one spadeful at a time.

Don't Miss

→ Gawking at postcard-perfect views of Sydney Harbour Bridge

→ Spotting old railway ties from the garden's former life

→ Seeking out the beloved Cupid fountain

Her death spurred her mother to garden even more fervently. The resulting sanctuary is a testament to grief and to the healing power of nature.

A joyful chaos

Thanks to public clamour, the rail company that owns the land has leased the garden to the local council, ensuring its protection (for now). Today, Wendy's garden sprawls luxuriantly down the hillside, tended by a small army of gardeners. Though not exactly a secret, it's still something of a hidden gem, known mostly

Find Your Joy

Getting there

Lavender Bay is 2 miles (3km) north of central Sydney. The garden is a short walk from the North Sydney or Milsons

Point railway stations or the Milsons Point or McMahons Point ferry stops. If driving, you can park at the adjacent Kirribilli Club. To find the entrance, look for the giant fig tree outside the four-storey house with the white tower.

Accessibility

The garden is on a steep hillside, with unpaved

paths and rocky stairs. Accessible views over the garden and harbour can be had from the fig tree in the upper tier.

When to go

September to November are spring, an especially pleasant time in the garden.

Further information

• Free admission.
• Open year-round.
• Dogs welcome.
• No cafe on site but picnics welcome.
• www.wendyssecret garden.org.au

Other Secret Urban Gardens

St Dunstan in the East Church Garden, England

This millennium-old Norman church was rebuilt by Sir Christopher Wren, only to be crushed during the Blitz. Today the ruins sprout moss and ivy, and the floor is carpeted in grass. There are benches to sit on, and, in spring, a profusion of bubbly hydrangeas. Amidst the skyscrapers of central London, it's a cool, calm, hidden oasis.

Don't miss
Having a picnic lunch on a warm day

St Luke in the Fields Garden, USA

In the middle of New York City's built-up West Village, this church garden is a charming surprise. Slate paths lead through a fairyland of rose bushes, cherry trees and birches, irises and tulips, surrounded by brick walls that retain heat and create a microclimate. Its first planting was a piece of England's sacred Glastonbury thorn, back in 1842.

Don't miss
Swooning over blooming cherry trees in April

Journey through horticultural history and fantasy in Hamilton

 Garden design, variety, colour

 November

NEW ZEALAND

Turn a corner and you're in an Ancient Egyptian temple. Turn another and you've stumbled into the Italian Renaissance. Another passage leads into a Mughal prince's palace, a Tudor knot garden, or a sustainable suburban backyard. The highlight of Hamilton Gardens is its set of 17 enclosed gardens, cleverly designed so that visitors can traverse them on a loop. Secluded behind hedges or walls, the gardens surprise and delight at each bend.

Heaven on Earth

Hamilton Gardens officially opened in 1960 but it wasn't until late the following decade that the seed of the current concept was planted. Rather than replicating other botanic gardens, Hamilton instead opted to create themed gardens, exploring garden design through the ages.

The gardens are loosely split into three 'collections'. The Paradise Garden Collection illustrates different cultures' conceptions of an Earthly paradise in garden form, ranging from a Sung-dynasty Chinese Scholars' Garden to a California-style Modernist Garden. The connection between gardening and art is examined in the Fantasy Garden Collection, including a Surrealist Garden with moving branches and eminently Instagrammable oversized objects. The remaining five fall into the Productive category, with a Kitchen Garden that will have backyard horticulturalists green with envy.

From one garden to the next you're never sure if you're going to be hit with a great wallop of colour or a

Right: Figure of fun? Papagano, the Bird-Catcher, greets visitors to the Picturesque Garden

Below: Tudor knot gardens are designed to be viewed from above; the joyful Indian garden

© NATALIACATALINA.COM / SHUTTERSTOCK

© ARTAZUM / SHUTTERSTOCK

© HAMILTON GARDENS

Hamilton Gardens

luxuriant crop of silver beet. It's overwhelming and inspiring in equal measures.

Kiwi culture

Two of the gardens have New Zealand themes. A wooden palisade decorated with carved representations of ancestors of the local Māori iwi (tribe) encloses Te Parapara Garden, named after a *pā* (fortified village), which once stood nearby. This Productive Garden demonstrates traditional agricultural techniques. Specialist gardeners from the iwi use the stars to determine planting and harvesting times, as their forebears have done for centuries.

Part of the Fantasy grouping, the Mansfield Garden recreates the setting of Katherine Mansfield's *The Garden Party*, the most famous short story by one of the nation's most celebrated writers. It's an oddly guilty pleasure, suddenly finding yourself gatecrashing an uppercrust Edwardian occasion.

Opposite: Up, up and away to Wellington Botanic Garden ki Paekākā

Right: Hamilton's Italian Renaissance Garden reflects the style's order and symmetry

© NATALIACATALINA.COM / SHUTTERSTOCK

Stretch your legs

The Enclosed Gardens make up only a tiny portion of the overall complex, which spreads along the Waikato River and includes a playground, an off-lead dog park and a Victorian-era cemetery.

Having opened in 1972, the Rogers Rose Garden is one of the earliest sections to have been laid out, and come November it erupts with colour and fragrance. After the sensory overload of the themed gardens, there's simple joy to be had in spreading out a picnic surrounded by such blooming beauty.

Don't Miss

→ **Drowning in colour in the Indian Char Bagh Garden**

→ **Searching for fantastical beasts in the Tudor Garden**

→ **Stumbling across the Russian bell tower near the Camellia Garden**

Find Your Joy

Getting there

The number 18 bus from the city centre stops a 5-minute walk from the gates. Limited services stop in the gardens.

Accessibility

Most of the themed gardens are accessible by wheelchair, and wheelchairs and mobility scooters are available for hire (book ahead). The fully accessible 'Changing Places' toilet includes a shower. A free accessibility map lists distances for those with limited walking capacity.

When to go

Maple trees fill the Japanese Garden with autumn colours in April and May. The Rhododendron Lawn, Kitchen Garden, Mansfield Garden and English Flower Garden are at their best from September to November. November also brings the Pacific Rose Bowl Festival to the Rogers Rose Garden.

Further information

• Free admission.
• Open year-round
• Dogs welcome on a lead, except in the enclosed gardens.
• Cafe on site.
• www.hamilton gardens.co.nz

Other North Island City Gardens

Auckland Botanic Gardens
Covering 156 acres (63 hectares) of South Auckland, these expansive gardens include a large tract of remnant forest and interesting displays of threatened native foliage. Seasonal delights include the spring daffodils and cherry blossom, the Rose Garden, the Camellia Garden and one of New Zealand's largest public salvia collections.

Don't miss
Being transported to the time of the dinosaurs in the Gondwanaland Arboretum

Wellington Botanic Garden ki Paekākā
Catch the heritage cable car up from the capital's main commercial street to the top of the country's steepest botanic garden and wind your way down the other side. Be sure to plan your route through the 62-acre (25-hectare) garden carefully, as you won't want to backtrack!

Don't miss
The seasonal flower beds at the Glenmore St entrance, especially in September when 25,000 tulips are in bloom

Escape to a cool mountain paradise

♡ Peace, stone walls and trees, Art Deco style

🕐 April and May

AUSTRALIA

The red, gold and yellow leaves chase each other along the paths and down the terrace, bringing smiles to the faces of visitors. The air feels crisp and leaves crunch underfoot. It's autumn at Everglades House and Gardens and there's no better place to experience the season's natural beauty. This haven of foliage and flowers is a garden created in the mid-1930s to surround an Art Deco-style house, and yes, there is a glade. Both house and garden have been preserved and are managed by the National Trust of Australia as examples of Art Deco and interwar design.

Grace and style
Situated in Leura, in the Blue Mountains west of Sydney, Everglades was a holiday home for Henri Van de Velde (1878-1947), who had a prosperous international business in felt and textiles. This region was favoured as a cool retreat from the heat, humidity and bustle of the city, and when Van de Velde snapped up the property – after the original cottage and garden had been destroyed by fire – he was keen to make the most of the location's panoramic views of the majestic Jamison Valley. Today those same views enchant visitors, gazing towards the sandstone cliffs of Kanangra Walls and Mt Solitary in the wild and remote Greater Blue Mountains Area World Heritage Site. Within the garden itself, sculptures, garden art and water features, including the Reflection Pond, accent

© NATIONALTRUST.COM.AU

Right: Spring at the Everglades: tulips have been a feature of the planting since the 1930s

Below: Garden with a view: take in the sublime Jamison Valley in the Blue Mountains

© RAMEEZ RAZA AMANULLAH / SHUTTERSTOCK

© NATIONALTRUST.COM.AU

Right: A spiral path leads into the rockery of the Blue Mountains Botanic Garden

Left: Walk this way for knock-out vistas of the Blue Mountains amid elegant greenery

Don't Miss

→ **Kicking fallen leaves**

→ **Rugging up and breathing in the crisp mountain air**

→ **Seeing the blue sky in the Reflection Pond and the breathtaking views beyond the garden**

the garden's layout. Wander further to explore the tranquil glade with its trickling stream and drifts of azaleas.

The house design is attributed to Eric Langton Apperly; the garden was laid out by Danish-born landscaper Paul Sorensen, and is one of his most significant creations. He produced a tranquil, restful space with terraces and low stone walls that tamed the natural slope and formed a series of intimate garden rooms. He planted banks of deciduous trees including Japanese maples,

silver birch and tupelo, and made grassed courtyards and private sunken gardens. The maturity of Everglades and the clean mountain air are evidenced by the moss-encrusted stonework and lichen on tree trunks here.

Grand but accessible

Today, Leura lies within commuter distance of Sydney but in the early decades of the 20th century, the area was favoured by the rich, who built large weekend residences set in lavish gardens. During the late 1930s and '40s, Henri opened his garden twice a year to raise funds for the Red Cross.

While Everglades continues to reflect the wealth, grand vision and passion of its owner, nowadays it's open to all and an easy day trip from the city. Rock up with a picnic and a rug and settle in on one of the lawns or perhaps find a quiet spot by the Reflection Pond for some restful contemplation.

Find Your Joy

Getting there

The nearest train station is Leura. The garden is a leafy 25-minute walk. It's also accessible by car, with free parking, or take the

hop-on, hop-off Explorer Bus from Katoomba railway station.

Accessibility

Much of the garden is not suitable for wheelchairs due to the slope, stairs and paths, however there is access to the top garden area. There's also seating and an accessible toilet on site.

When to go

The garden is known for its cherry blossoms, which are in peak flower in mid-September, along with wisteria, rhododendron and azaleas. Arguably the most glorious time to visit is from mid-April to mid-May when the deciduous trees put on a colourful autumnal show.

Further information

• Admission charge. Tickets can be purchased online.
• Open year-round, except Tue.
• No dogs allowed.
• Cafe on site and picnics welcome.
• www.nationaltrust. org.au/places/ everglades-house- gardens/

Other Blue Mountains Gardens

Blue Mountains Botanic Garden

Thriving in Mt Tomah's rich basalt soils is this botanic garden of cool-climate plants from across the globe. Highlights include waratahs, proteas, rhododendrons, masses of spring-flowering bulbs and blossom trees. Enjoy views from the visitor centre veranda across the bushland wilderness where ancient Wollemi pines were discovered in the 1990s.

Don't miss

Admiring the living fossil tree, the Wollemi pine, close-up

Mayfield Garden

This former sheep station has taken its inspiration from gardens of stately European homes. The central feature is a water garden with ponds and cascades set among terraces and sweeping lawns. Owned by the Hawkins family, the garden was planned as the family's retreat. The vision grew, as earth and rock were sculpted into an extraordinary horticultural experience.

Don't miss

Photographing the Stone Bridge flanked with maples

Soak up Tasmanian history among the plants

 Trees, calming views, roses

 November and December

AUSTRALIA

Stretching across a slope above the magnificent River Derwent in Hobart, capital of the cool-climate island state of Tasmania, is a site that brings together classical beauty, over 200 years of history and the story of the island's unique vegetation – the Royal Tasmanian Botanical Gardens.

Chances are you'll be welcomed by a volunteer who'll help orientate you, quiz you about specific interests and set you on your way to take a snapshot of Tasmania's indigenous flora, to discover the best seasonal blooms, or to find a place to relax and take in the views and tranquillity. As soon as you step through the gates, you'll feel welcomed and very much at home.

Repurposing and reusing

One of the gardens' appealing features is the embracing of older structures as well as plants. Much loved by wedding parties is the imposing Anniversary Arch – originally built in downtown Hobart in 1913, it was moved to the gardens in 1968. The Conservatory was constructed here in the late 1930s using stone recycled from the colonial-era Hobart Hospital. It features pots of lush ferns and palms and an ever-changing floral display of orchids and begonias.

Convict past

Hobart was established by the British in 1803 as both a settlement and a prison for convicts. The gardens started life as a vegetable plot providing food for the small colony, assuming its current role in 1818.

Right: Honouring the garden's heritage, the statue of a former gatekeeper works the garden

Below: High, convict-built brick walls create a shelter for roses; an eastern rosella visits

© ROYAL TASMANIAN BOTANICAL GARDENS

© ROYAL TASMANIAN BOTANICAL GARDENS

Q&A

What brings visitors to the RTBG?
Australians grew up watching *Gardening Australia* with TV gardeners Peter Cundall and Tino Carnevale working here, so many people want to see where the show was filmed. Word of mouth has put us on the map as well. Visitors tell me they've been told 'you have to visit the botanical gardens if you go to Tasmania.' So, they do and they're not disappointed!

What are your wow moments?
The trees – I absolutely love our huge old trees. I always tell visitors to look up, the trees are spectacular. Our ferns are rather lovely too. And people swoon over the roses. There's so much really.

It's not a big garden though, is it?
That's part of its charm. It doesn't seem daunting, and you get a good overview of the site as soon as you come through the gates.

Eileen Maskrey, Volunteer

© KIRSTY NADINE / SHUTTERSTOCK

Royal Tasmanian Botanical Gardens

Hobart's early governors left their mark, none more than Lieutenant-Governor Arthur, who had the high brick wall that surrounds the upper gardens built in 1829 using convict labour and handmade bricks. Known as the Arthur Wall, it was designed to be heated through a system of fireplaces, flues and chimneys. It's one of the few surviving walls of its kind in the world. Another lieutenant-governor, John Eardley-Wilmot, had an additional wall built along the eastern border. Today these walls help create a special microclimate in which plants thrive.

Stately trees
The oldest tree is a sprawling, centuries-old cork oak, and the gardens also hold the largest collection of mature conifers in the southern hemisphere, planted during the 'conifer craze' in the 19th century.

While the exotic tree collection dominates the skyline, around

Opposite: Crawleighwood Garden – the life's work of one couple

Right: The great cork oak dates from the mid 1800s and is one of many significant trees

© ROYAL TASMANIAN BOTANICAL GARDENS

30% of the plant collection is Tasmanian, including those housed in the world's only subantarctic plant house which exhibits flora from Macquarie Island, a remote island some 960 miles (1550km) southeast of Hobart in the Southern Ocean. Wrap up as this plant house is cooled to keep the plants happy, then warm up at the Lily Ponds. Dating from the 1840s, these ponds now have elegant circular wooden viewing platforms, known as the Lily Pads, which were added in 2018 to mark the gardens' bicentenary.

Don't Miss

→ **Hugging the nearly 200-year-old cork oak**

→ **Inhaling the scent of roses and lavender**

→ **Being dripped on by water beneath Tasmania's endemic tree ferns**

Find Your Joy

Getting there
The gardens are a 5-minute drive from central Hobart or a 25-minute stroll through the Queens Domain. Just beyond the imposing gates of Government House is the shady, tree-lined entrance with its impressive iron gates.

Accessibility
The gardens' excellent network of all-weather paths has some steps. A buggy tour, ideal for visitors with disabilities or tired tourists, is available (booking required).

When to go
The gardens are beautiful year-round as the horticultural highlights change according to the seasons, but November and December stand out as the peak time for roses and perennials.

Further information
• Entry by donation.
• Open year-round.
• No dogs allowed.
• Restaurant, takeaway kiosk and gift shop on site.
• www.rtbg.tas.gov.au

Other Tasmanian Gardens

Crawleighwood Garden

South of Hobart stands this flourishing private garden open to visitors. In what were once weed-covered paddocks, this space has been developed over four decades to showcase cool-climate trees, and shrubs and plants from the southern continents. Wander among rhododendrons and climb the grassy hill to enjoy the view of the forest that surrounds the garden.

Don't miss
Having a chat with owners Pav Ruzicka and Penny Wells

Patterdale

Colonial artist John Glover captured on canvas Tasmania's landscapes and inhabitants in the early 19th century. He also painted the garden he created around his home, Patterdale. The property's current owner and landscape designer Catherine Shields used Glover's 1835 painting *A view of the artist's house and garden* to recreate the original layout with modern twists.

Don't miss
Exploring 'Glover Country' and other locations the artist painted

© CRAWLEIGHWOOD GARDEN

Find form in an English-style garden

NEW ZEALAND

Bay views, sculpture, regeneration

November

Any day is the perfect day to visit Ōhinetahi, just south of Christchurch on New Zealand's South Island. With its enviable position overlooking the cerulean water of Governors Bay and its wealth of horticultural and historical interest, this award-winning garden is sure to put you under its spell.

A garden through time

When the first European owners erected a cottage here in the early 1850s, they adopted the Māori name Ōhinetahi. Meaning 'place of a single daughter', it had been used by an earlier family with lots of boys and just one girl.

A decade or so later, Thomas H Potts, one of New Zealand's early European botanists, built the sandstone homestead and established vegetable gardens, an orchard, plus exotic trees and shrubs, some of which still stand on the grounds. After Potts' death the garden was neglected for nearly a century – until, in 1976, the property was purchased by Sir Miles Warren, his sister Pauline Trengrove and her husband John. The new custodians were confronted by an almost derelict house, a few surviving trees and a large lawn to the west of the house (today a favourite picnic spot), but Miles and John brought their skills as architects, and Pauline added hers as an artist to create something extraordinary. Aiming to revive and improve the site, they sought inspiration by visiting some of Britain's best gardens – the idea for Ōhinetahi's Tower came from Sissinghurst in southern England, while

Right: Virginia King's *Heart of Oak* sculpture peeps through the ferns

Below: Shades of red and green mingle in the walled Red Garden; a place for reflection

Q&A

Ōhinetahi sounds like a good name for a song?
It could be a contemplative song about an only, precious daughter and the beautiful garden sharing her name.

What's your favourite aspect of working here?
Many elements combine to make the whole place, and together they make the place whole. I love them all.

Who or what inspired the design?
A garden was first planted here in the mid-19th century but became derelict. It was crying out for attention so two architects and an artist, drawn by the amazing location, answered the call. A stunning garden was developed.

Ross Booker, Garden Manager

Ōhinetahi

the Red Garden was influenced by Hidcote's Red Border in the Cotswolds. The trio settled on a structurally complex design with a series of garden rooms around two perpendicular axes. There's an Arts and Crafts-style formal garden, a sculpture walk and a woodland trail where established trees provide protection for regenerating native plants.

Perhaps it's the architectural influence, but the garden's balance of form and shape give a sense of satisfaction. And combined with the luxuriant herbacious borders and displays of roses, rhododendrons and camellias, the feeling turns to rapture. It is unsurprising that the New Zealand Gardens Trust awarded Ōhinetahi their highest six-star rating.

More than just plants

Ōhinetahi is also renowned for architectural works, sculptures and art galleries. Over two dozen exceptional pieces,

Opposite: Modern cultivars and heritage roses can be enjoyed in Christchurch Botanic Gardens
Right: Andrew Drummond's *Astrolabe* takes in the views of Governors Bay

positioned throughout the garden, encourage you to pause for reflection, while the galleries inside the homestead hold the works of New Zealand artists.

Developing the garden gave the two architects the perfect counterbalance to their professional lives – here they felt it was OK to make mistakes, though none are noticeable, and their relaxed attitude is reflected in the welcoming feeling. Sir Miles bequeathed Ōhinetahi to the nation in 2012 and now visitors can be inspired to create their own garden sanctuaries.

Don't Miss

➡ Climbing the Tower for a Sissinghurst-inspired overview

➡ Photographing the Ruin, a folly along the sculpture walk

➡ Staying calm on the swing bridge across the fern tree-lined gully

Find Your Joy

Getting there
Driving is the only way to get to the garden. It lies 9 miles (15km) south of Christchurch. The drive takes you across the picturesque Port Hills mountain range.

Accessibility
Wheelchair users have access to flat areas around the main house, but most of the garden is not accessible for people with mobility issues.

When to go
There's an abundance of floral delights in spring (September to November) and summer (December to February) which also offer the best chance of good picnic weather. The many trees in the garden make sure autumnal hues don't disappoint come March and April.

Further information
• Admission charge.
• Open September to April.
• No dogs allowed.
• No cafe but plenty of scenic picnic spots.
• www.ohinetahi.co.nz

Other Gardens near Christchurch

The Giant's House

In the historic French township of Akaroa, southeast of Christchurch, stands this quirky garden where whimsical, masterfully crafted mosaics cover everything from steps and walls to the multitude of sculptures. The owner, Josie Martin, has participated in artists' residencies around the world and is renowned for her creative flair and horticultural expertise.

Don't miss
Seeing what's on display in the Contemporary Art Gallery

Christchurch Botanic Gardens

In a city of many green spaces, the Botanic Gardens stand out as one of the most beautiful. Grand old trees, from cool climates and temperate Asian areas, anchor the sprawling setting along the Ōtākaro-Avon River. There's something to see in every season, though the heritage roses and impressive herbaceous perennials are November and December highlights.

Don't miss
Seeing New Zealand's only World Peace Bell

Fall under a tropical spell in Cairns

 Plant education, peacefulness, lush foliage

 July to September

AUSTRALIA

Come into the garden, our titan arum wants to see you. Haven't heard of it? When this quirky, 155lb (70kg) giant of the plant world is in flower you'll soon know, thanks to its unforgettable, rather smelly florescence – hundreds make the pilgrimage to see and sniff it. Luckily, many of the other 4000 species growing in Cairns Botanic Gardens are more sweetly fragrant – a welcome counterbalance – and some are amongst the world's rarest.

Instant appeal
Your awe-inspiring visit begins when you step through the wrought iron gates featuring Licuala palm fronds. Once past the shady lychgate (a perfect shelter from tropical storms) you emerge onto a peaceful swathe of lawn. It's time to take a deep breath. Palms with dramatically patterned trunks and towering trees – some planted in 1886 when the gardens were first established – embrace this sun-soaked patch. It's a foil for the abundant beds filled with verdant foliage and colourful blooms.

Nature's class
There's no right way to explore the site. You could follow one of the paths through the Gondwanan Heritage Garden and learn about the evolution of plants. Or head to the Aboriginal Plant Use Garden where signage explains how myriad plants were, and often still are, used as 'bush tucker' (food and medicine) by Australia's original inhabitants. Many

Right: Into the rainforest to experience what Cairns was like before settlement

Below: Among the garden zones is a freshwater swamp with water lilies, frogs and turtles

© AUSTRALIANCAMERA / SHUTTERSTOCK

© ALEXANDER JUNG / GETTY IMAGES

Q&A

What makes Cairns Botanic Gardens so unique?
Nestled between the Great Barrier Reef and ancient rainforests, the gardens showcase a huge range of exotic and native tropical plant species.

It's a 'wet tropics garden'. Do you work in a jungle?
It's wet. It's tropical. In places, it's a jungle too! There are manicured and open areas as well, so many parts are highly cultivated while some look wild.

Where's your favourite spot to hang out?
The Conservatory in the morning when the fogging system is on. It's quite surreal when plants appear out of the mist, then disappear back into it again.

What animals live here?
All creatures great and small. Orange footed scrub fowl and brush turkeys rake mulch and detritus into mighty nest mounds. Bandicoots, pademelons, lizards and snakes can be shy, while birds and butterflies are everywhere.

Charles Clarke, Botanic Curator

indigenous plants seen here are now familiar in domestic gardens, and some are produced commercially. There's lots to absorb.

Green on green

Turn right instead at the entrance gates and you can follow a path crossing a stream to the Rainforest Boardwalk. It's a circuit and not too large so there's no chance of getting lost – however appealing that might seem in these gorgeous, green surroundings. The plants here originate from both Australia's northern rainforests and other tropical regions, but species of palms, gingers, orchids, bamboos, vines, aroids and tropical fruit trees look like they've grown here, together and happily, forever.

Almost central to the gardens is the Watkins Munro Martin Conservatory, also based on the design of a local *Licuala ramsayi* fan palm. It houses a significant collection of rare plants including

Opposite: King of the jungle? The surreal and fascinating Paronella Park

Right: Keep an eye out for pademelons emerging from the forest at dusk to graze

© LUKE SHELLEY / SHUTTERSTOCK

understory tropical palms, cycads, ferns, nepenthe, pandans and orchids. Butterflies love it as much as humans.

Treat yourself

Now you'll need coffee and cake, or delicious lunch in a cool spot. Two restaurants, both cocooned amongst heavenly flowers, are the perfect places to enjoy delicious fare beneath breezy fans. Come for breakfast and chat to local regulars, then head out to explore knowing that no matter how hot the day is, it'll be degrees cooler amid all the greenery.

Don't Miss

➙ Spotting plants and butterflies in the Conservatory

➙ Learning in the Aboriginal Plant Use Garden

➙ Listening out for the early morning birdsong

Find Your Joy

Getting there

Cairns Botanic Gardens is situated on Collins Avenue, 2.5 miles (4km) north of Cairns' Central Business District. Catch a Sunbus which stops at the gardens' entrance.

Accessibility

Apart from some paths in the Flecker Garden section which are not suitable for wheelchairs and prams, the whole site is accessible.

When to go

Visit any month and it feels like the garden is putting on a show just for you. In love with heliconias and gingers? They're at their best from July to December. Orchids your passion? Visit from May to September. Insect-devouring pitcher plants are ravenous in January and February.

Further information

• Free admission.
• Open year-round.
• No dogs allowed, except registered assistance dogs.
• Two on-site food outlets.
• www.cairns.qld.gov.au/experience-cairns/botanic-gardens

Other Queensland Gardens

Paronella Park

Magical and mysterious come to mind in this surreal park, an easy day trip south of Cairns. In the 1930s, Spaniard José Paronella had the idea of building a castle in the rainforest. The resulting dream-like creation is a mix of architectural curiosities and tropical flora, with waterfalls and fountains thrown in. Start with the tour and let your imagination lead you from there.

Don't miss
Seeing what's on display in the Contemporary Art Gallery

Brisbane Botanic Gardens Mt Coot-tha

Located on Brisbane's western edge, with Mt Coot-tha looming above, these gardens treat visitors to a global botanical adventure with sections covering places such as Japan, Central America and Africa. The highlight has roots closer to home – the world's biggest collection of Australian native rainforest trees.

Don't miss
Following the circular path up through the Tropical Display Dome

Index